MORE ABOUT THE SPIRIT WORLD
AND
EXPERIENCES IN ASTRAL PROJECTION

MORE ABOUT THE SPIRIT WORLD

Being a further collection of personal experiences during conscious Astral Projection, followed by A Treatise on The Electro-Magnetic Basis of the Spirit Body and its faculties.

By
FREDERICK C. SCULTHORP

Author of "Excursions To The Spirit World"
(Now in its Fourth Edition)

Published by
The Greater World Association Trust
3 Lansdowne Road, Holland Park,
London W11 3AL, England

First Published 1975

© *The Greater World Association 1975*

This Edition 1982

ISBN 0 900413 37 9

Made and Printed in Great Britain by
The Garden City Press Limited
Letchworth, Hertfordshire SG6 1JS

CONTENTS

INTRODUCTION

Mr. Sculthorp is a fascinating writer, he writes simply and naturally, and his book "Excursions to the Spirit World," first published in 1961 has had a world-wide appeal. The subject is unusual, but of vital interest to all since each one must pass into that "Other World" sooner or later, and the descriptions which Mr. Sculthorp gives of his visits there during physical consciousness opens the vision to these tremendous possibilities of the Future Life. Mr. Sculthorp has the remarkable faculty of vacating his physical body during the day, and bringing back a full recollection of what he has seen and heard while in the Spirit World and the people he met there, including his own wife. They are happy encounters. Mr. Sculthorp is a religious man and links his philosophy with these out-of-the-body experiences in a way which will help many to overcome their doubts and fears about the Hereafter, and comfort those who mourn, for these pictures are of a happy continuing life, of reunions and retained memories of the earth-life.

The author has also an advanced scientific mind, which he brings to bear upon the construction of worlds from their atomic particles and explains the physical and spiritual worlds from this angle. This is contained in a wonderfully interesting "Treatise" which comprises the second part of this book.

This is a remarkable work—a worthy successor to "Excursions To The Spirit World," and the reader is assured of an informative introduction to the curious subject of Astral Projection.

A. H. Hillyard.

EXCURSIONS TO THE SPIRIT WORLD
REVIEW BY MRS. ELLA SHERIDAN

The name of Dr. Karl Müller of Zürich is internationally known to Spiritualists and psychic researchers as that of a scientific observer of wide experience. He did more than any other person in propagating the truth of survival and spiritual return in Switzerland and for several years (since the transition of David Bedbrook) has been President, as well as Research Officer, of the International Spiritualist Federation.

Mr. Frederick C. Sculthorp is as yet, unknown, but I venture to predict that, as the author of a new book, "Excursions to the Spirit World" (to which Dr. Müller has written the Foreword and an Appendix, which takes the form of a general Survey from the historical and scientific angle), published by Almorris Press, Ltd., it will not be long before the name of F. C. Sculthorp will be known and respected by many people.

As the title suggests, the book tells the story of travels in the astral, in this case, the author's own experiences. We have had, it is true, other works dealing with the subject, recently the erudite work by Dr. Crookall and much earlier works by Sylvan Muldoon, Hereward Carrington and others. These are valuable, but unlikely to attract the casual reader, in fact, they are more in the nature of text books. "Excursions to the Spirit World" is a straightforward record of Mr. Sculthorp's conscious "out of the body" travels. The language is simple and direct and the experiences are related with extreme clarity.

I had the privilege of reading the manuscript and was immediately impressed. I have since read the proofs several times, but it is true to say that I never became bored, but retained my interest throughout and, each time, I discovered some new point to ponder upon. Every "excursion" stands alone and yet there is a continuity which makes the book as easy to read as a novel and much more interesting than most.

What has struck me, and is perhaps the most important factor of all, is that every single incident described brings out some particular lesson or aspect of spiritual law, so that the reader is gradually and pleasantly initiated into the philosophy of the spirits. In this alone, the book is completely different from all the other works concerned with astral projection which I have come across. When it is realised that Mr. Sculthorp was not a Spiritualist nor interested in the matter until after the passing of his wife and presumably knew little or nothing of Life on the Other Side as known to Spiritualists, his experiences, which confirm so much of what we believe, are surely all the more convincing.

It would be difficult to give an idea in a mere review such as this, of the scope and implications of the records. Various planes of activity were visited, the differing states of spirits are pictorially described and the reasons explained, demonstrating the Spiritualist contention that each individual reaps what he sows.

There is one reference which I feel must be mentioned here as it is one which is likely to appeal to our readers especially. On page 120 Mr. Sculthorp, in a very touching and revealing chapter, tells his readers how he was brought into contact with the spiritual presence of Jesus. He says, "I am not a religionist and I have never voluntarily attended an orthodox church service, so my study of different beliefs was in the nature of a sincere quest for truth." He goes on to relate a vivid experience and how he became aware that Jesus is "in charge of the world." Some time later quite unexpectedly, through the mediumship of a psychic artist, he received a sign that seemed to confirm his experience. During the early part of the Second World War the "traveller" visited a plane where he saw a Figure which he says he *knew* was Jesus, although He was unlike any of the traditional portrayals of Him. After that experience Mr. Sculthorp tells how he came across the inspired picture by

Bertha Valerius (The Living Christ) and at once recognised it as a good likeness of the Master as he saw Him.

In the Introduction, Dr. Müller tells how the book came to be published and writes of his own enquiry into the subject of astral projection. His Appendix is a scholarly and informed survey of the whole question which has occupied him for many years.

I consider this book outstanding because of its simplicity and manifest sincerity as well as for the teaching which is evident in every "excursion." To be read by the beginner and the converted alike.

COPY OF A BOOK REVIEW IN "THE CHURCHES' FELLOWSHIP FOR PSYCHICAL STUDY"

(March, 1962. No. 31)

Excursions to the Spirit World, by Frederick C. Sculthorp, with introduction by Dr. Karl E. Müller. (Almorris Press Ltd.)

The author tells his remarkable story of how his faculty of conscious astral projection developed, enabling him to visit the Spirit world and bring back clear memories of his experiences.

His experiences cover a period of more than 20 years, and his descriptions of the scenes he witnessed during his excursions comprise a wealth of detail and make absorbing reading.

A clear insight is given into the similarities and also the differences of life here and in the Beyond. The language is simple and direct and the experiences related with extreme clarity and manifest sincerity.

Dr. Karl Müller gives a survey of the subject from an historical and scientific angle.

EXCURSIONS TO THE SPIRIT WORLD
REVIEW BY MRS. P. M. WADSWORTH

Many readers will be familiar with this exceedingly valuable little book (published by the Greater World and advertised often in the newspaper), but it is new to me and I feel it important enough to write a review, to bring it to the notice of new members, readers and friends who may not have had the opportunity of making its acquaintance. I do not think I have read any book on this subject of astral projection which makes so profound an impression of utmost sincerity, simplicity, humility, together with a sense of reality one cannot ignore.

It is quite simply written, but every word, every sentence "pulls its weight," to give the overall picture of others worlds, other realms, both of lightness and darkness; some to which one might hope to go—others one fervently hopes to be spared from visiting!

Mr. Sculthorp is in no wise daunted by any of his adventures, but proceeds with what I feel admirable serenity, learning a great deal from these strange occurrences, adding his succinct comments—and, if I may say so, his love for all humanity both on this side of the veil and on the other.

I would advise anyone interested in spiritualism and astral projection to make sure of a copy while the stocks last.

FOREWORD

We sometimes read accounts of people under an anaesthetic during an operation, who have found themselves floating over their physical bodies and even visiting other parts of the hospital, then, on regaining consciousness, have related certain incidents and had them corroborated by those in attendance.

This free floating body, composed of certain elementary particles and invisible to physical sight, is the spirit body and is not affected by gravity.

It is the inheritance of humans and all living things; there are no exceptions—"To-day thou shalt be with me in Paradise!"

I have had these experiences in this floating or "spirit body" for over thirty years and it is called "astral projection" or "out of the body" and projections were from an armchair or bed.

They were not haphazard, but were conducted by a gentle and spiritually advanced man who lived during the Ming Period. Like all who are in the higher planes of Spirit, he is under the leadership of Christ.

Apart from a few earthly experiences, my travels were to the Spirit world and I have writen about them in the book *Excursions to the Spirit World*.

This booklet consists of articles I have written from time to time, and explains certain happenings more fully.

I hope it will be helpful to many, especially to those who have experienced the dreadful sadness of losing a loved one, as I have done.

"Blessed are those that mourn"—I used to wonder what this meant. I know now, for mourning is love, and love is the greatest of God's laws, and in my case provided a link and I was blessed beyond my wildest dreams.

Nothing is lost, for Spirit is timeless, and the past is present between loved ones—who, "wonder of wonders," remain in the prime of life.

I am not a churchgoer—the compulsory church parades in the army during the first world war, and the absence of any trace of brotherly love quite put me off. There are many gentle ones in the Spirit realms who work with the help of the Master. Just ask for your spiritual needs—you know how.

FRED. C. SCULTHORP,
Jones House,
Bentham, Cheltenham.

ASTRAL PROJECTION

I have now experienced astral projection for over 30 years, and as all the travels, except for a half-dozen or so, were to the Spirit World, it has given me a little knowledge of spirit life and an inward happiness because all life continues. No yearning for reunion is unanswered, even with our animal friends. Some may think that in the intervening period before the reunion in spirit something has been lost, or perhaps that loving companionship has waned with the years. That is not so. All memory is contained and held in the spirit body which encompasses the physical body on earth. The physical brain is simply the "detector" (in the electronic sense) of that memory, and as we all know, age can dull that physical organ. In the sensitive spirit body memories of the past are there with all the details, and there is no physical impediment, therefore "the past is present." To emphasise the significance of this, "time" as we know it is absent, and the companionship continues, but with intensified happiness because love emanates from the surrounding auras of two spirit friends meeting, causing the further upliftment of both. The spirit message we often hear, "I am very happy," can mean more than the actual words convey, as I very well know.

Many on earth with the desire for knowledge will later be amazed at the wonderful effects of the spirit laws, if they are willing to listen to the spirit teachers.

What the Master taught (and He lived according to His teaching) can be better understood and with this understanding the mentality becomes clearer and open to further knowledge.

The increase of knowledge of physics, radiation and electronics is helpful and the physicists know that everything has a rhythmic pulsation or vibration of different frequencies. It is hard to define the borderline of physical and spiritual. The coloured butterfly which finds the buddleia blossom, or the moth that can find its own species even miles away, can be an up-wind sensing of molecules, yet one must realise the delicacy of the antenna and the sensing of the rhythmic frequency of the molecules.

I have found that in the spirit world water can flow, is buoyant, and can be drunk, but it does not wet my spirit clothes if I enter it.

The free particles of all atoms gravitate to the magnetic belt surrounding the earth and form the familiar localities and countries which one sees in the first spirit planes. As they are of different atomic structure, all places on earth have a different frequency of vibration, and this is so with the counterpart of the localities in the Spirit World. A person passing over from this country would not go to a Chinese or South American part of the Spirit World, as the spirit body is inured to the vibration frequency of his own country. An analogy is the mystery of the adult salmon which, even from a vast ocean, is drawn back to the same river of its spawning. It is simply because no other place has that frequency of vibration. Let us hope that the search for knowledge flows over the border from the physical to the spiritual. I have before me a cutting taken from the "Daily Telegraph" some time ago.

"By Our Science Staff"

"The announcement of the American Atomic Energy Authority of the discovery of the Anti-X1-Zero particle is of particular interest to astronomers. . . . The idea of anti-particles gives rise to some fascinating possibilities. It is quite conceivable that there might exist a kind of looking-glass world, in which all matter is made up from anti-matter. Life in such a world would be exactly the same as ours. For all we know such a world might well be in the far-distant parts of the universe."

HAPPY REUNIONS IN SPIRIT

(Although the spirit body feels normal and "solid" it is composed of elementary (electric) particles, and immediately responds to thought. A progressed spirit can travel, when needs be, at great speed.)

I had projected at night and was taken to a bright plane in spirit, which denoted a progressed state.

I was alone on a vast grassy plain, and as I waited expectantly and looked at the beautifully clear surroundings, I saw two pin-points of light far away in the distance.

They seemed to get brighter and then suddenly became two brilliant orbs of blue-white light which were travelling towards me at a tremendous speed. Before I had time to be startled, they stopped before me and became two young men. They were two of my army companions of the 1914 war who had passed over and made good progress in spirit.

Their appearance was very fine and bright and I sensed their extreme happiness in meeting me and their thoughts contained a wonderful flood of benevolence and companionship which rather touched me. I in turn was also tremenously happy to see them which no doubt they also sensed, and we excitedly recalled our former times together on earth.

We chatted for a while and then said "Goodbye" and as they started to go, one suddenly turned back and kissed me on the cheek, and then rejoined his companion. I was not surprised—I knew that his progressed state held the sincerity and tenderness of real brotherhood and the kiss meant more than he could express in words.

Much happiness is felt in the sensitive spirit body when meeting friends in spirit. In this meeting, when I saw my companions, I was naturally happy to see them and radiated that thought. In turn, my friends' pleasure in seeing me, emitted a similar thought which infused my spirit body with further friendship towards them. This interchange of thought passes back and forth with mounting intensity and speed and is cumulative, so much so that all the dross of earth life is forgotten and I felt intensely happy to be with them.

This is the spirit effect of God's laws, for what is given out is returned a hundredfold, and the feeling of companionship and closeness was much greater than we ever felt towards each other on earth.

How much more so does this law take effect when meeting one's marriage partner in spirit?

Zodiac says in "Marriage and the After-Life": "True

it is that there is no 'marriage' in the bright spheres but there is a unity between soul and soul which far transcends anything that has ever been experienced, even under the most ideal conditions upon earth." ("The Greater World," January 12th, 1963.)

What is it that "far transcends" anything on earth?

In the earthly body it is difficult to imagine the finer sensibility and feeling that pervades the spirit body, and after many years of experience of life in the Spirit World, I find it equally hard to describe it.

If meeting my army companions in spirit gave me such happiness, the reunion with my wife in spirit was certainly beyond all earthly happiness. In the mingling of auras we knew one another's thoughts, and there was a blend of affection which was far beyond earth and biological reasoning. The union of tender and sincere thoughts made us good "conductors" to the influx of the ever present "God stream"—it was almost overwhelming, and we wanted nothing more than the bliss of one another's company.

Spiritual things must be spiritually discerned and spiritual feeling can only be felt in its fullness in the spirit body. An earthly analogy—if one is moved by a beautiful melody, would be to imagine that feeling magnified a thousand times and shared by one's beloved.

"And when they come Home, they will find their loved ones waiting for them, and in that reunion—which means a unity which is impossible to explain in words, because it is of the Spirit and not of the body—joy and perfect happiness becomes their own." (Zodiac.)

(The teacher from the Spirit World, "Zodiac," quoted at times, is the one mentioned in St. Mark's Gospel, 12, 28-34. He spoke through the mediumship of Winifred Moyes from 1921 to 1951.)

A TEA-PARTY IN THE SPIRIT WORLD
(Lovely people—lovely children—and a lovely party. And to book lovers, a hint of future joys.)

I had projected during the night and met my wife (who had passed over) in a house full of ladies. As well as the great happiness, as in all our meetings, it was very pleasant to be with these people as it was a progressed plane. All the ladies were busy, and I sensed the preparation for a party or celebration. A newcomer entered, a lady with a basket containing a parcel, and someone said, "It's the Queen," but I did not recognise what past queen she was.

I went with my wife to another room, and presently she said she would help the others to prepare some dishes. Left alone, I saw a book on a table and sat down and casually turned the leaves.

The book dealt with furniture, flower arrangement, etc., of a home in spirit, and the position of windows and their outlook. As I saw the illustrations and read the paragraphs, I became enveloped in a strange happiness—a warm welcome —and I realised that my sensitive spirit body was psychometrizing all that the spirit author had impressed on the book. The picture of a comfortable room would emit a wonderful warmth of welcome. A window would become a panorama of beauty showing sunny lawns bordered by flowers, while the mind of a great friend seemed to draw one to share its beauty with him. My casual look at this apparently ordinary book had turned to a delightful happiness—in fact, I almost lived in it! I suddenly sensed the presence of my wife and looked up.

Knowing my interest in books, she had turned back to see the effect it had on me, and stood smiling. I said to her, "What a wonderful book. I wonder if I could get one like it?" "You will," she said. I got up and we went into the room where the others were, then I lost consciousness. (Consciousness often waxes and wanes during a projection, but the "higher self"—the finer spirit body—still carries on.) Becoming conscious again, I found that the "tea-party" was nearly over and I was finishing a trifle of fruit and jelly which was rather nice. We all went to another room where there were about 20 tiny children. The eldest I should think could not have been more than three years old, and they sat in a group on the floor with the smallest ones in front. I noticed that several of these small ones had a delicacy of features and a tint of clothing that was ethereal and "different" and I had the impression that they were stillborn babies.

My wife began to tell them a fairy story. Then followed what was, to me, one more delightful experience of a happy state in spirit.

These children were very beautiful and their little faces were upturned and rapt in a happiness of wonder and delight as the tale unfolded. On this plane the mind of the story-teller has greater clearness and scope which can envelop their little minds with unspoken beauties, and even mental pictures connected with the fairy tale. When the tale ended my wife said to them, "Now we will go into the next room to see the fairy's treasure"—and they went off happily singing a nursery rhyme which I had not heard before, but it was a happy tune and beautifully sung, as is usual in spirit when minds are in unison.

The children returned, still happily singing, but I began to lose interest—my time was up, and I returned to the bed and switched on the light. As I looked at the clock—it was near 2 a.m.—I was impressed about something concerning the date. I thought for a few seconds; it was April 24th, my wife's birthday, and so the well-kept secret was out—it was *her* birthday party!

Later, a medium friend said to me, "Do you know that you tell fairy stories to spirit children?" I did not know it, but I am certain my wife does!

(Note: Psychometry is handling an article and sensing the thoughts of the owner. The ultra-high frequency of the owner's thought emissions causes an induction, which is held by the article.)

CHILDREN IN SPIRIT

She was a little girl of about ten years of age and as we walked, I had my arm around her and my hand on her shoulder. I thought her dress (spirit robe) was rather long, but I was upset when I saw that she had bare feet.

As I had "mothered" *my* two little girls, when my wife passed over, I felt sorry for her shoe-less state. But I need not have worried, for the little girl had the situation well in hand. She was leading *me* on my first conducted tour of the Spirit World.

Zodiac has often spoken of the work the spirit children do, and some may wonder how a child can help an adult with a lifetime of "knowledge." As the spirit body retains *all* life's thoughts (one can ponder over the millions of thoughts in an adult mind) to deal with a situation, the past memory is probed for that knowledge, and the solution, when found, is probably an earthly one!

A child, who passes over at a very early age, has not this mass of thought, and in its innocence has a spirit body that is appropriate to a higher plane or wavelength in spirit.

As the plane and its people are advanced, everything it learns is truth and in its innocence accepts everything and speaks truth. It forms a lovely personality devoid of fear, worry or doubt, and to be close to the aura of such a child gives one a feeling of serenity and quiet happiness.

One Sunday afternoon, I had projected from an armchair and was taken to the bright countryside in spirit with park-like scenery of trees and grassy slopes. I saw several people sitting on a bench and I went and sat next to a little girl, who was sitting close to a man. I sensed that she had spent most of her life in spirit, and she began to talk to me. She was a lovely child of about seven years of age and spoke simply and clearly, and in her conversation mentioned Jesus.

As our auras were mingling, I sensed a connection and asked her if she had seen Jesus lately. In a quiet matter-of-fact way she answered, "No. He is now on duty in the East." (It was April, 1961.) The man sitting on the other side of the little girl was a neatly dressed office-type, and being with this little girl, I thought he would know quite a lot. I leant forward and asked him, "What do you think of life after death?"

To my surprise he at once stiffened and adopted an earthly conventional pose and replied in a dignified tone, "I do not wish to discuss the matter." I immediately knew that he was one of the many still living in a dream-world, or what has been called "The Plane of Illusion." He did not know that he had "died" and was now in the Spirit World, and the little girl was patiently waiting for an opportunity to help. I tried to think of some possible line of talk, despite the rebuff. I saw a movement beside me, and turned. A lady, who was sitting by my other side, was rubbing her brow and seemed to be thinking deeply. She murmured as if to herself, "That's strange. Now I come to think of it, the river Exe (Devon) doesn't look the same." My journey arranged by my spirit helpers was evidently not altogether fruitless, as my thoughts had some effect on the lady. It is rather strange how those still connected with earth (like myself) can sometimes bring enlightenment to a spirit, and in a rescue circle it will be noticed that a spirit brought for help, will often become conscious of the new state by simply contacting the thoughts of the people in the circle.

Spirit children are often taken on sight-seeing tours in the Spirit World, and on one occasion I was out-of-the-body and with my daughter who has passed over. We were watching a long line of these children. They looked the same as children on a school outing, and I picked up one little girl and said, "And where have you come from?" and she said, "Venezuela." I asked her, "Are you tired?" Her eyebrows went up in bewilderment. "No," she said.

My daughter was laughing. It was a silly question, as I knew there was no physical tiredness in spirit, but my earthly thoughts immediately connected such a journey with fatigue, hence the child's surprise.

PERSONAL INTERESTS IN THE SPIRIT WORLD

During astral projection to the Spirit World I have seen many of the earthly interests of people still being enjoyed. In the bright states these are only part-time, as that state is only reached by helping the others less progressed. It is God's law that in helping the welfare of another, "self" is absent and is replaced by the purer God-power, and this the Master taught in various ways. I have previously mentioned my daughter in Spirit who on earth enjoyed horse-riding, and still does so in the Spirit world. At other times she teaches children and classes of young people. My father enjoyed his garden on earth and on one projection he showed me a room in his house in spirit that was full of flowers like a greenhouse. It looked beautiful as the walls seemed to admit all light. On one occasion I was helping him to prepare the garden of a house in spirit for a newcomer.

I said to him—"and we can hide that shed with a row of runner-beans." He was very amused and I realised that there were more colourful flowers in spirit than scarlet runners.

There are orchestras and brass bands in the spirit world and I have played an instrument, and have found it much easier as the fingers respond at once to thought. I should think that it is easier to learn an instrument in spirit as the mind is clearer and retentive. I have seen and enjoyed small boat sailing, and there are also ball games. In some bright states, however, one can direct a ball by thought, so there would be no point in having a competitive game. My spirit teacher once took me to a lower state where there were people watching a football match.

When the ball narrowly missed the goal, I said to the man near me, "That was close," and he agreed and seemed pleased to be spoken to. With my attention on the game again, he edged closer and entered my aura, and I sensed he was a pickpocket! I felt a slight touch towards my coat pocket and I said, "You won't find anything there." Immediately the nimble fingers were withdrawn and were fondling the lapel of my coat, and quite unabashed, he was saying, "I used to have a suit like this." This is the mentality and ignorance that enters the lower states, and one wonders with sadness as to what possible way of approach can be made to help.

I visited a park in a pleasant state in spirit which had several buildings which many people were entering. Each building had something of interest, including all the arts, mechanical, printing, etc. One small building had a narrow circular canal which ran through one side and out the other. Inside there were boys playing with model boats, and I said to one boy who was watching his model liner sail by, "What makes it go?" "Vibrations," he replied with gusto and was evidently pleased to expound something a spirit teacher had told him. It was amusing to hear this word being used by one so young, yet it is the basis of all states and all activity. Last year I again met my wife's parents in the spirit world.

It was a happy meeting and I was glad to see them as they are a cheerful couple, and they were pleased to see me. But the meeting had been arranged, for they presented me with an ebony walking stick! (It was a sign that they knew that walking now tired me on earth.) It was also another spirit lesson for me for when I left them I still felt the pleasure of their friendship and company, and I realised that my sensitive spirit body had a continuous psychometric impression of their personalities in the stick I was carrying! This is another pleasure we can look forward to in spirit— a present always carries a reminder of the donor's personality.

THE MIRACLE OF SPIRIT AND MATTER (1)

"Everything in physical life has its spiritual counterpart."—ZODIAC.

During astral projection to the spirit world I was once talking to one of the teachers, who drew my attention to my clothes. I saw I was wearing my usual suit; it even had a small stain on it, the same as its earthly counterpart!

All atoms have "off-shoots"; electric particles which have the same vibration as the parent atom and therefore the same "sensation" or property, but in non-physical form. So even the stain had to conform and have its replica of off-shoot particles. The significance and magnitude of this must be realised, as a grain of sand has its spiritual counterpart, therefore the desert, countries, continents, seas, oceans—everything! This spiritual counterpart has no weight and is not affected by gravity, but is held by the magnetic zone surrounding our planet. During astral projection the magnetic zone (aura) of my spirit body attracts the spirit counterpart of my earthly clothes because they hold my personal vibrations. *All is vibration.* Different localities and countries have different atomic composition and mass and therefore different vibrations. Racial minds have their certain "traits" which is also a vibration, but it is not generally noticed by the slower physical senses. The spirit body is very sensitive and during a projection to the spirit world, two unprogressed and sadly deformed people were brought to me, and I knew their nationality by their emissions (vibrations).

The ultimate basis of spiritual and physical things is elementary particles. *Free* elementary particles of different frequencies (fine or gross) also permeate all space. (Some physicists say 100 to the cubic centimetre.) In the unimaginable vastness of endless space, in which our Earth and Sun are mere specks, there is enough "material," if concentrated, for many new worlds. ("Zodiac" denies the astronomers' theory that the earth and moon were thrown off from the Sun.) In the spirit world spirits can form spiritual things by the concentration of positive thought (electrical activity) on these negative free particles, thus bringing them together.

I have been in the lecture rooms in the spirit world where many subjects are taught, and spiritual science is only one of them and is for those who wish to know. However, having a knowledge of spiritual science or not, those good souls who empty themselves of "self" and extend friendliness and help to others, find that their "giving" is replaced by further powers and a pure happiness. When I have been taken to them in the bright planes I have felt their radiations, and it seems that by their friendliness they have become "good conductors" to that God-stream of power, the greatest law of spirit—and simple too, "Love one another." The Man who entirely eliminated "self" had a love and compassion for others to such an extent that He and the God-stream are One. In His earthly life His mysterious miracles were for all to see, but His teaching was simple. The instructions are still simple—too simple for the wiseacres, but they are true and direct, and if all acted upon them there would be an accumulated and unhindered stream of power that would transform the world.

Many years ago when I was "seeking," He once told me that He was "in charge" of our world. I treasure the memory of His presence and His simple statement, for like the sparrows, even I and all of us are "known."

THE MIRACLE OF SPIRIT AND MATTER (2)

("Homing," which is a mystery to biologists and other scientists, is no mystery in the spirit world. A spirit can easily "home" on to his old earthly residence, and to loved ones on earth—there are no Sign-posts in Spirit!)

How did the dove find its way back to the ark? Its home was mobile and not localised! It is a Bible story, but the peculiar homing happens to-day. A pigeon fancier related the following:

A man in London bought a pigeon from one in Staffordshire. He kept it for a time in his pigeon loft, but when released it did not return. He wrote to the previous owner, who said that the bird had returned to him—*but,* he had moved to Wales. The pigeon had not returned to its previous district, but to its old familiar loft now in Wales! "Zodiac" often mentioned "vibrations" and it is often the subject of lectures in the spirit world.

All is vibration. Solids, liquids and gases have different vibrations in the atoms composing them. Our God-given senses can recognise different foods and liquids by the frequency of the vibration of their atomic composition. The same applies to light rays; different frequencies have different colours. Our senses can detect the invisible free floating molecules forming odours which, too, have their vibrations. Everything has electrical association; the atoms with their electrons, our bodies composed of atoms, and our nerves conveying the vibration or "sensation" to the brain.

The electrical activity of the mind can be recorded by an instrument and contact, but positive thought has a frequency of many millions and far beyond the sensitivity of an instrument yet made. If such a thought has "desire," as in telepathy, the radiation is far-reaching, even penetrating mountains and the curvature of the earth as if they were non-existent.

The pigeon previously mentioned, whose personal vibrations were already impressed on its old loft, radiated a yearning thought for "home"—contacted it and thus found the direction.

Some years ago a daily paper reported the incident of

a farmer in Devonshire who took over a farm in Scotland, taking his cat with him. In four weeks the cat returned to its old home "very much the worse for wear." This was no haphazard wandering and the route must have been direct for such a journey. A London evening paper had a brief report headed "A Mystery." A cow whose calf had been taken and sold at a cattle market, got out in the night and found its young one. It was on a farm 30 miles away. On its journey it had to cross the river Thames—"no one knows where!"

The loving mother had yearned for a very personal belonging—her treasure and found it. I have often wondered if they were allowed to be together again, if only for a time.

Another vibration in the "Miracle of life and spirit."

IF THEY ONLY KNEW

After living a double life for over 30 years (sounds like an old lag's confessions in a Sunday paper) I have often been saddened by a casual expression, a paragraph I have read, or something mentioned on the radio. My "double life" is the continual visits I have made to the Spirit World where the results of our earth life are plain to see.

I have just heard on the radio ("What The Papers Say") that better organised bank raids, etc., and the technology, can even be learnt by these men in prison, who prove that crime does pay. *All crime is paid for.* The reporter who seemed to admire this "skill" will later be appalled by his earthly ignorance.

The minister of a small church spoke about his shrinking congregation—sometimes only three or four attending—and said that his living really came from the people of the past who left money to the church and who are now "sleeping in the churchyard." If the minister had shed some of his theology and in his heart "became as a little child" he would find that the Master will amply reward his "seeking." And if he finds that there are no sleepers in his churchyard, but active and friendly people in their new life willing to come and help him he could teach this in his church and lift the hearts of many.

If his "sacrifice" causes a few lifted eyebrows, the cross in his church should remind him of that greater sacrifice and the hatred and jeers of proud priests of that time.

The news today seems to be a repetition of robbery, violence and vandalism, all of which will have to be paid for later in the dreary twilight states, and I have seen no clever ones who have "got away with it."

It is not news but it is a fact that the great majority of people in our country are well-ordered and friendly, and many are surprised on entry to the next life.

The unnoticed (so she thinks) mother who has attended to the home, the many cares of the children, the family wash and that ever recurring "washing-up" has done something for others. She does not think of reward or even thanks. She has done something without thought of *self*, which is the great law of spiritual progress. The Mary's and Martha's are blessed!

Money, fame and titles have all gone and those who have grown into the habit of privilege have many adjustments to make. Only the real and personal character is left. If only they knew!

"JOE MORLEY"

My "excursions" to the spirit world are not often now, but not long ago I had an experience that gave me pleasure and was also surprising and evidential. Years ago there used to be a concert player, Joe Morley. He was a solo banjoist and I had seen him at Kensington Town Hall, and he also played at Wigmore Hall and other places. He was well known and very popular among the fretted instrument players, both for his playing and his many compositions. Morley passed over some years ago at a good age. One afternoon from my armchair and out-of-the-body, my spirit teacher took me to see Joe Morley in his spirit life. Morley never knew me on earth (I was just one in the audience) but the meeting gave great pleasure to both of us and he was beaming all the time. I like these happy meetings in spirit, for when the auras intermingle the pleasure is reciprocal and greatly intensified far more than earthly feelings.   Although he was old when he passed, he now looks 35-40, with the healthy-looking and fine features of spirit.   Before I left him, I congratulated him on one of his fine compositions, "El Contrabandista," and said, "I suppose you often played this at concerts," and Morley said, "No, I never played it publicly."

This surprised me, and later I wrote to the Assoc. Editor of "B.M.G." (the monthy magazine for Banjo, Mandolin and Guitar) asking if he or any of his friends had ever heard or known Morley play his own composition, "El Contrabandista."   He replied, neither he nor his friends had known him to play it.   I thereupon told him the reason for my enquiry and my meeting with Joe Morley.   He very kindly gave a full account of my experience in the February issue of "B.M.G.," which I hope gave pleasure to those who knew this old player—*and* to the spiritually younger Joe Morley.

AN EXPERIENCE IN ASTRAL PROJECTION

(This is a strange experience.   Zodiac tells us that the human spirit was created in God's Image, and that animals are a separate creation.   This gentle human entity apparently never incarnate, and from another plane in spirit, may have used or controlled the spirit body of the foal in order to learn with the children, in preparation for earth life.)

Note: My wife's parents and their forebears were country people.   Her father had a lot to do with horses, and when they came to live in London, he still kept his own horse.   He was a kindly man, but was not interested in Spiritualism, and passed over with no knowledge of spirit.)

Out of the body, I became conscious in the back room of a big old farmhouse.   I was with Doris, my wife, who had passed over, and sensed that it was the home of her father in spirit.   Doris asked me to bring in a saddle which was hanging outside, and I took it into a part of the house which was the big living room.   Inside, I saw her father, and also to my surprise, there was a young foal which was walking about the room. It was a lovely creature and although long-legged, was well formed and had beautiful eyes.

When I went forward it turned and saw me, and my appearance startled it and made it restless. However, as is usual in spirit, it at once received my friendly thoughts and was quite calm when I stroked its fine silky coat. My father-in-law told me that he was looking after the foal and it had become a sort of household pet.

I spent a considerable time, the whole projection, in and around this house, with many periods of consciousness waxing and waning, and was often with this beautiful animal, and it also seemed to like my company. Now comes the strange part of my experience. When I was alone with this foal, I could sometimes clairvoyantly see and apparently superimposed at first a young human entity. At times when my power was greater, the young horse would entirely disappear and I would see the complete form of a young person who would sometimes speak a few words. The entity appeared to be about 15 to 17 years of age, and I sensed a gentle nature of neither sex.

I was bewildered and went and found my father-in-law. I had to be cautious as I had the impression that he could not see what I could see, and I said to him, "That young foal of yours seems to be very knowing." He replied, "Yes, it is. That is because it mixes a lot with young children, and is being brought up with them."

I could sense that he knew nothing more than this, and after I left him I was given the vision of the foal actually being with children when they were having spirit lessons.

Once when with the foal and it was speaking, I gave it some simple sentences to say and it repeated them perfectly. (I could not bring back to my physical mind the words that were spoken, but I remembered that I gave three sentences of simple words to be repeated.)

On another occasion when I was sitting at a table the foal approached, and I sensed that it had an intense desire to write. It was rather pathetic and I felt touched by this simple yearning to be like other humans, and I thought, "How can a hoof hold a pen?" Immediately I clairvoyantly saw two finely formed spirit arms held out appealingly as if wishing to make the effort.

By this time I had been a considerable time out-of-the-body, and I felt a waning of power. There was also some activity in my home as it was tea-time, and I was in an armchair in the living-room, and I was unwillingly drawn back to earth.

In my contact with this entity, I felt an innocence and tenderness that had never experienced the material things and hardships of our world, and I am wondering if I have been shown this gradual transformation or metamorphosis that takes place.

THOUGHT AND MEMORY IN THE SPIRIT WORLD

(A knowledge of the spirit world through the literature now available in this country can be a treasure above all earthy values. The wiseacre's "one world at a time" is always regretted later.)

One of the many things that impressed me most after many visits to the Spirit World by astral projection was the effect of thought.

Naturally, in the first planes of spirit this concerns the earthly thoughts that people bring with them. Each is an individual whose only "possession" is a lifetime of thought which the spirit body holds.

Memory, like many other things, is taken for granted, yet a moment's reflection will make us realise that *nothing can, or has ever happened* without a cause. Thought is generated electrical activity, and like all electrical movements, has a vibration frequency and pattern which is impressed on the living entity, therefore there is a retention of that thought which constitutes a "memory" always at hand. This can be realised when a competent psychometrist handles an article belonging to a person and "senses" outstanding episodes in the life of the owner, because the article has been impressed by the magnetic patterns. I stress these incidental "mechanics" of thought as it is generally overlooked on earth as we are all living on the same plane, but in spirit the effects of thought are clearly apparent.

In the spirit world we do not suddenly become "all

wise" as we have only our store of earth memory, but if it contains some knowledge of spirit truth, the reality of survival, and a way of life accordingly, then the mentality is not incredulous and opens in a wonderful way. The spirit plane of new arrivals is near the same frequency of vibration as the spirit body and is quite earth-like, and for quite a time some good souls cannot understand that they really *are* in the world of spirit. On one occasion in the spirit world my spirit teacher took me to a small group of people.

They were evidently told that someone was coming to talk to them as they were smiling and seemed glad to see me. There were about eight of them sitting on chairs, and I sensed that they were not aware that they had "passed over," and were living in what is sometimes called "the plane of illusion." I knew that to bluntly tell them their state would only bewilder them, so I tried another method. I went to each one and whispered, "What day of the week is it?" Each was puzzled and amused at their uncertainty and named different days. The last one, an elderly lady, thought for quite a time without result, laughed and thought it was her usual bad memory! Anyway, it was a start to make them realise that they were now in a place where there were no "days of the week," and what was more apparent, no nights.

I have a daughter in the spirit world and on earth she was fond of horse riding in Epping Forest, near London. During one projection my spirit teacher took me to a nice country house in spirit just as she was returning from a ride. We chatted for a while, then my daughter asked me to wait as she wanted to see a friend in the house.

I was rather worried about her horse as there were flower beds, and it had walked off. I found it round the back of the house on a grassy part with some other horses. I noticed that her saddled horse had a nice smooth coat, but the others were unclipped. It is indeed hard at times to realise that one is in the Spirit world, and Zodiac emphasises that there is nothing on earth that has not a counterpart in the bright realms. My daughter was wearing her usual riding clothes, and she once told me that she has a special robe which she wears when taken with groups visiting higher states.

I have ridden a horse in spirit and I wrote about it in "Excursions to the Spirit World." It is an experience I have not forgotten, for if one is really an animal lover and not interested in them because they win races or competitions (or because they provide handy targets for shooting) love directed at a horse is returned "full measure and brimming over" and can actually be felt in all its fullness. I have found this so myself.

Zodiac tells us (forgive me for quoting him again, but he is always right) that the horse is the nearest animal to man, it has toiled through the ages for man, and in spirit can still love mankind. Thank God for everything—including horses.

THE "HIGHER" SELF

Zodiac has often mentioned in his messages that many leave the body during sleep and go to the Spirit World, but the experiences cannot be remembered as the subconscious mind is of a higher vibration or frequency than the physical senses. Some spirit teachers call this "The Higher Self" and it can have a higher vibration than the spirit body used in astral projection.

I have had fleeting experiences of this higher self during astral projection, and on a few occasions it has been prolonged for certain reasons. In "Excursions to the Spirit World" I mentioned the lectures I attended in spirit but could not recall the actual teachings because of this higher frequency of thought.

In later projections I used to be somewhat perturbed on return because I had been speaking to spirits on subjects that I had no recollection of learning in spirit, but I now know that the higher self can remember all experiences and teaching.

On one occasion I was with my wife at a social centre in the Spirit World. I saw Arthur Conan Doyle and introduced him to my wife. I never knew him on earth, yet at the time of the introduction I knew that I had met him before in the Spirit World.

He is a fine figure of a man and his shoulders seemed to

fill the doorway. I was surprised to see how fair he is; his pictures on earth do not show this.

I once knew a lady who had seen the nature elementals around flowers, and my daughter in spirit had also seen them. As she described them as "diaphanous" I thought it would be a long time before I would be able to see them. However, a few weeks ago during a projection I was with a small group by a pool in the Spirit World, and I saw one of these elementals among some rocks. It was about a foot high and had a small red coat like a soldier's tunic, and I explained to the group that they loved colours and were fond of imitating humans. Later I wondered as to what authority I had for telling the groups this, but I "knew" something about elementals at the time through the experiences of my higher self.

Once I tried to influence the subconscious mind of one who had visited the Spirit World during sleep. I had projected and was with my wife who had passed over. We were in a room in spirit and I was surprised to see that her sister, who is still living on earth was with us. I thought it would be a good opportunity to show her the reality of spirit travel. I said to her: "Now you know that Doris (my wife) died, yet here she is with us." There was no reaction, she just looked blank and began to rearrange some books on a table. I looked at my wife and she smiled rather sadly; it had been tried before without success.

The different levels of thought are quite separate; my sister-in-law could see her "dead" sister, could handle books, yet was quite unconscious of a spirit reality.

Turning to something more definite. In February I projected one night and met my father in spirit and he told me that Lottie (my sister living in London) had something wrong with one of her legs. I wrote to her about it and she replied, "Thank you for your nice newsy letter. It is amazing—I have a thrombosis in my leg. . . ."

MORE ABOUT THE SPIRIT REALMS

In my out-of-the-body experiences in the Spirit World I have often been taken to cities where life goes on just the same as on earth. There are shops with their shop-assistants and people looking in the shop-windows. There are hotels, theatres, railway stations with their goods yards and people working in them, which was evidently their calling when living on earth. One theatre was very striking; the palatial front of it (there are no building costs in spirit) was so overdone that I thought it looked like a wedding cake!

These cities are all overcrowded and their emanations are not uplifting to the sensitive spirit body. Naturally, these city experiences surprised me in my early travels, as I was also taken to other places which were beautiful parklands which were bright and sunny, and simply to be there gave a feeling of continuous happiness and the people I met were full of peacefulness and true friendship, and no one was a "stranger."

Gradually I learnt the cause of the overcrowding of these cities. The people in them were orderly but they still had the same thoughts as on earth. They were happy enough to exist as they have always done and had no idea of better spirit states.

Although I have mentioned these apparently normal cities in spirit, I have been to others that are gloomy, and some almost like twilight in comparison with the brighter states. When I was walking in one of these cities, I noticed a lady on the other side of the street who looked quite bright. She wore a long white dress like the classical Greek style and looked very graceful, and I was surprised that the inhabitants took no notice of her. I then realised that she was a higher spirit there for some purpose, and that she would therefore be invisible to them. Later, I wished I had spoken to her, but I did not like to intrude. I did not like the feeling in this state and levitated above the house-tops, where I went through patches of mist or fog. One patch was of inky blackness and I felt apprehensive, until I suddenly sensed the presence of my spirit teacher and felt quite cheerful in spite of the gloom. I never understood the fog patches above the streets of these lower towns.

Visiting these crowded cities in spirit leaves a sadness when I think of the many who make no progress. They appear to be of all classes of people, from the modern matter-of-fact person to the Victorian crossing-sweeper I saw, still humble and obsequious, and the Jacobean inn-keeper still with his knee-breeches and buckled shoes.

Those who know of spiritual facts and *try to live accordingly* are indeed fortunate, for the same mentality is carried over to the same frequency in spirit, which is brighter than the materialistic mind state. That is why I mentioned the earth-like quality of those cities in spirit, for the people there cannot readily be approached concerning the happier states with any more success than on earth, and many of us know how futile that can be.

"Unless you become as a little child" is simply being willing to learn entirely different "data," the unchanging spirit laws. A string of earthly academic honours can be an inhibition in cases where pride is unconsciously held.

Those who are well acquainted with spiritual literature may have read of the "Halls of Learning" in the spirit states, and I have also mentioned in "Excursions to the Spirit World the lectures I have attended in spirit. This may sound rather wearisome, especially if one is elderly, but they are in the bright states and the spirit body does not tire. In a more recent projection, I was taken to a large building and felt bright and uplifted. Inside, it appeared like the vestibule of a high-class hotel with thick carpeting, and round the walls were plush-covered settees on which people were sitting. As I passed through it, somebody got up and joined me. It was my wife! The happiness of meeting a loved one in spirit cannot be fully expressed as the auras of each mingle.

We went over the building where the corridors were also thickly carpeted and stopped at an open door of a room where a lecture was in progress. I looked for the lecturer, but no one was addressing the people and all were looking at an instrument on a table. It had an upright wheel over which there was a "chain" of oblong tablets linked together. When I looked at the instrument (the spirit body emits a ray or surge of enquiry) I gathered that it was delivering a lecture, with each tablet containing a subject and, of course, ready for use when required—a kind of spirit tape-recorder. I have also seen projected pictures on screens for lectures or entertainment, which were perfectly stereoscopic and three dimensional.

The many interests in the bright states are unlimited and I think that an interest in many subjects during earth life (and not a one-track mind) can be an advantage later on.

We have been told to "Follow"—we have been told the "Way." Let us help each other on that way.

BEYOND PHYSICAL SIGHT

Many years ago a man used to come to my shop during his lunch-hour for a chat. He was a welder in a local factory and one day I asked him what would happen if he kept his oxyacetylene flame continuously on a block of steel.

He said, "It would gradually burn away."

"What about the ashes?"

There would be no ashes. It is the hottest gas flame known and burns everything."

"Where has the steel gone?"

He made a gesture, "In the air—dispersed."

"Then we are breathing it?"

"I suppose so—some of it."

"Where has the weight gone?"

(The subject was then abruptly changed.)

*   *   *   *

Research into the fundamental structure of matter has proved that "solid matter" is, in reality, not solid in its basic constituents. The atoms have been found to consist of a bewildering number of "particles" which are nothing more than concentrations of energy. Matter and energy have proved to be interchangeable.

The principles of wave-mechanics have revealed that the sub-atomic particles behave as though they were nothing more substantial than trains of electro-magnetic waves.

*   *   *   *

It was many years ago when I met that fine medium, the late Mrs. Helen Spiers, at the Marylebone Spiritualists' Association (now the Spiritualists' Association of Great Britain). Her accurate descriptions of my wife and other relatives and their characteristic personal messages, which became a sort of family conversation, amazed me.

It was my first experience and I asked, "Can you actually see them?" for I could see nothing. She smiled and said, "Yes, and you will see your wife as clearly as you see me now." How true this was when later an advanced spirit teacher took me on out-of-the-body journeys to the spirit world. I attended lectures there, sometimes with my father, and for this reason I started this article with the two anecdotes, which have an association.

In astral projection my spirit body is composed of sub-atomic or elementary electric particles, and of course unseen to physical eyes, although I feel "solid."

A sunbeam in a darkened room will reveal dust, but not electrical particles.

All space is saturated with these free sub-atomic particles, and well distributed, as being negatively charged they repel one another. Those in spirit, according to their state of progress, can construct spiritual things by thought— the thought being a positive electrical emission, attracts the negative particles. Therefore, the basic ingredients of *everything* spiritual or material is in space around us in the form of free particles.

Only One on earth had the great and far-reaching attractive Power "The Father in Me" to bring together the substance and forming by thought a repetition of loaves and fishes.

EXCURSIONS TO THE SPIRIT WORLD

During the early hours of the morning of Sunday, October 24th, I found myself looking at a vast empty hall in spirit.

I sensed that it was in one of the intermediate states where people had not been very long in the spirit world, and that there would be a great gathering of people to see Christ, Who would appear. I went out to the surrounding roads and saw many people approaching and marching in orderly fashion, like a town's carnival parade.

They were in companies, each company representing their different countries or races, and all looked happy and expectant. One company, all ladies, looked very happy.

They were all wearing the same style of dresses which were rather long and white. They looked very graceful and all had nice features.

When I was suddenly taken back to the great hall, I had the (earthly) idea that there must be a reception committee somewhere, and entered an ante-room, but it was empty. Before I could leave, a man entered—an old-aged pensioner. He seemed to represent many old people; slow walk, slow speech, clothes carefully tended—the need for thrift and care in living.

I was amazed. All the thoughts and cares of an elderly person were being impressed on my sensitive spirit body—yet *I knew he was the Master*. I have seen Him before, but not like this, but His emanations are unmistakeable. He knew my thoughts and smiled and said, "I have dispensed with my beard, to be more in keeping with these modern times." (I described the colour of His beard in my book.)

He continued to talk slowly, but I was too dazed to remember, but He said, "The churches could use the post office for their savings," and I replied, "I expect some of the small ones do."

My consciousness comes and goes in spiritual experiences, but the next thing I knew was to find myself in the vast hall watching a great assembly of people. I was behind them and all were intently staring forward, when a lady turned, ran to me looking happy and excited, kissed me, and then rushed back to her place in the crowd. She was my sister-in-law, and I noticed that my brother was with her, but he was too intent to notice anything else. Then, unfortunately, my time was up and I returned to my bed, so I do not know in what form the Master appeared to the people. (My brother and his wife have not been in spirit many years. She followed him in 1962.)

* * * *

We publish by way of explanation the letter from Mr. Sculthorp, covering the account of his experience.

24th October, 1965.

Dear Mrs. Sheridan,

I am sending the enclosed account of an experience which happened last night—or rather in the early hours this morning, Sunday, October 24th, hoping that you may hear of any of our friends who may have also attended in spirit, or have some recollection of it, when awakening this Sunday morning.

The sister-in-law mentioned, who has passed over, had a vision of the Master when on earth, and she is also the one who gave me the remarkable proof of telepathy, as related in my book (page 116).

Needless to say, when I arrived back in my bed, I was full of this visit of Jesus to an intermediate state and the vast concourse of people there. My meeting Him and the circumstances and remarks, may seem strange to some, but those who follow Him must know that the Greatest can be humblest, and can be with any of us—know all about us, and put us at our ease like a great friend.

I am the Secretary of the old people's club "The Good Companions" at a nearby Cotswold village. They are good companions and I like them all, which may make the experience clearer.

If you should have any spirit impressions when reading the account, or any corroboration, I should be glad if you would let me know.

F. C. SCULTHORP.

THAT INDESTRUCTIBLE BODY (1)

An earthly incident. . . . I used to have a stationer's shop and, as I also sold newspapers, it had the usual frames outside for posters. In bed one night my spirit teacher detached my spirit body and rushed me outside my shop. I saw that a small van had stopped. A man got out and with a brush and paste can quickly applied a poster. Shopkeepers had often complained about this "fly-posting," but I was also annoyed to see that he had covered a poster that was of local interest. The new poster belonged to one of the national daily papers and had on it "Winners For To-day's Big Race." However, I could do nothing about it and drifted back to bed. I sat up and turned on the light and saw that the alarm clock had only 15 minutes to go, so I got up.

As I was putting the kettle on for some tea I was

impressed that the offending poster *would still be wet,* so I went outside and neatly peeled it off!

I could sense the amusement of my spirit teacher and wondered what the busy editor of the newspaper, a man eager for news, scoops and big headlines, would have thought had he known of that incident.

The wise and gentle "man in charge" who teaches me lived during the Ming Period (1400-1500 A.D.) and never heard of the Nazarene when on earth. He is now an advanced worker for Christ. When he is with me in the Spirit World —and has not reduced his "light"—it is like trying to look into the sun!

We never know how often these bright ones leave their beautiful spirit states to be with us in our daily lives.

THAT INDESTRUCTIBLE BODY (2)

I have often wondered what would be the outcome if one of our expert physicists in atomic science got up from his armchair and in his spirit body (as I have done) walked through the closed door of his room, although he felt perfectly "solid."

If he told his colleagues he would have to be very patient with them. (Like telling primitive men that the firm ground they are standing on is turning at the rate of a thousand miles an hour, and also hurtling through space at many thousands of miles an hour.) If he should dare tell them that his spirit body is composed of physically invisible particles they would demand to know their identity— mesons, positrons, protons, etc. (which they have also never "seen") .

But what of this body that can go through the solid wood of the door? He would have to remind them of their early lectures, for that solid wooden door is mainly space, and if its atoms were magnified so that the nucleus in the centre is as big as an orange pip, the nearest surrounding particles would be 40 feet away (and that is space indeed!) The sublimate particles of the spirit body have no difficulty in passing through the widely separate "barrier" of the physical door.

THE "NATURAL" SPIRIT WORLD

Zodiac's statement that there is nothing in physical life that has not its counterpart in the spirit world should always be remembered, and those who have no inkling of this fact cannot understand the earth-like appearance of everything when they pass into the next life. It is so natural that during astral projection to the spirit planes I often forget where I am.

On one occasion I was following a pretty little brook which, reaching a rocky part, formed a small pool and then went underground.

Swimming in the pool was a frog, and fearing that it might get carried underground—and forgetting that creatures in spirit cannot get harmed—I tried to catch it so as to put it in a safe place. It easily eluded me (spirit creatures cannot be "caught" but only attracted by a friendly thought) and in my last grab for it my sleeve went under the water. When I withdrew, my hand and sleeve were quite dry and I remembered I was in spirit.

The elementary particles of the spirit state are not molecular and water has not the affinity and does not cling or saturate. It is like putting one's finger in mercury on earth and not being "wetted" by the mercury.

Some years ago I read that the theatre in the district I was born was being demolished, and I had nostalgic memories of the pantomimes I saw when a child, and later went there with my wife. My spirit teacher evidently got my thoughts and a day or so later I projected from my armchair and was taken to see it still existing in the spirit world. I was delighted—there was the old "Palace," but just as new looking as when it was built, despite its long life, for there is no smoke in the spirit state to begrime it. I aproached it and read the play-bills, but I did not recognise the entertainers' names and thought I might trace them later. I felt in my pocket for pencil and paper to note them down—when I realised that not even a piece of paper can be *brought back* to earth! Such is the nature of spirit life as Zodiac tells us, "The counterpart of physical things."

A few months ago I was taken to quite another sort of theatre in spirit. It was not a "town" theatre, but was in a bright plane in park-like surroundings and was for purely amateur use. The people were very friendly, like a family gathering, and there was no criticism, no professionals, and anybody could try some amateur talent. They even tried to get me to join a party on the stage, but I said "I can't even *sing.*" But they said, "Never mind, stand in the back row." But I demurred, as I didn't think I would improve the scenery. One little girl gave a solo ballet dance and suddenly stopped in the middle—she had forgotten her steps and was very crestfallen, but was at once surrounded by loving ones and was soon all smiles again. When I was strolling round the building, I suddenly had a telepathic call from my wife with all her personality and love. Excitedly, I looked in that direction, and in the distance on a grassy slope I saw three ladies and knew that one was my wife! I ran towards them, but on reaching the spot there were only two. They were pointing—there was my wife, she had drawn a little apart so that we could talk alone!

How can I describe meeting a loved one in spirit? We have been meeting in the Spirit World for over 30 years, and that love is not only deathless but increases, for the radiation of love is *squared* in its intensity, and that is God's mathematics and God's greatest law.

But far better is Zodiac's description, "In the Bright Sphere . . . there is a unity between soul and soul which far transcends anything that has ever been experienced, even under the most ideal conditions, upon earth."

ANIMALS IN SPIRIT LIFE
AND ALL THOSE UNWANTED PUPPIES

How instructive are the teachings of Zodiac on spirit life. Recently reading one of his addresses, I noticed that he mentioned that not all animals have a perfect spirit body on entry into spirit life.

I have never seen this in print before, and it may be perplexing to some. During out-of-the-body experiences in the spirit world, I have noticed this with dogs, as some are unlovely and have snout-like noses. I believe that in the domestication of thousands of years they have a **natural** attraction towards humans, and when they are **driven,** beaten, unwanted and unloved, especially in those **countries** where there is little food for humans—not to speak of **stray** dogs, their daily wretchedness has left its mark.

However, they have their compensations in spirit life and will improve, for it is very wonderful how animals in spirit can at once feel a human's thought or aura of affection.

On one occasion in the spirit world, I looked over a low wall and saw a dog with puppies. She at once sensed my friendly thought and came to be fondled, and to my amazement—followed by an army of puppies! There must have been a hundred of them, large and small, all following "mother." The big ones were in front and trailed out to the smallest babies, who could barely wriggle along. It was a strange and moving sight, and yet another spirit lesson for me. The many puppies which pass over need mothering and the environment of maternal thought and love, which the spirit "mother" was only too happy to give.

"Not a Sparrow falls—"

"YOU WILL NEVER SEE DEATH"

During out-of-the-body experiences in the Spirit World, I have seen many who have recently passed over but are unconscious and remain so for varying periods. I have also seen some regain consciousness and I am told that I help in this respect. This surprised me at first, but it seems that as I still belong to the physical world, my mental vibrations or emanations are nearer to the new arrival and so stirs or animates the senses. It is somewhat like the members of a rescue circle whose spirit knowledge emanates and brings enlightenment to a spirit brought for help.

There is no surprise at first or dramatic awakening, nor would it be logical to expect them to say, "Oh, I thought I was dead," for we have often "dozed off" during an illness and we are not surprised when we wake. One day we will lose consciousness and awaken in the Spirit World, and serene, like the little girl who woke in my arms and said,

"Can I have a drink of water?"   It is God's law and we
should be thankful that the actual detachment is painless
and natural, for our real home is the Spirit World and our
span on earth is but a lesson to be learned.

Perhaps the most casual awakening in spirit happened
when I was standing with some spirit helpers round a man
who was lying on a table.   He stirred, sat up, swung his legs
round and slipped off the table, and rather hurriedly walked
through the doorway, as if he had been found sleeping in a
waiting room or some such place!   The morbid thoughts in
earthly minds concerning death are not to be found in the
Spirit World as they are negative and against the spirit laws.

Years ago, my sister-in-law's neighbour passed over.
He was a member of the local church (Congregational) and
the day after the funeral, another member of the church met
my sister-in-law.   She had attended the service for him at
the church and was rather shocked.   Experiencing spontaneous clairvoyance, she had seen him there and he said
rather gruffly, "What is all the fuss about?"

THE MIND OF CHRIST

Those who have studied the communications and
teachings from Spirit have perhaps read that some are taken
to higher planes to see the presence form of Christ.   The
vast congregations at these meetings may number
thousands, yet *each one* separately and simultaneously
receives from Christ encouragement and help in his or her
own personal progress in spirit life.   This is the mind of
the Master and something we are unable to understand until
after eons of spirit experience.

The greatest earthly minds cannot really grasp the
significance of outer space which extends *for ever,* and the
galaxies which gradually dim in the distance for millions of
light-years and *still* continue.   Zodiac and other spirit
teachers tell us that this Earth is "a speck among many
specks, and beyond these many specks is a vast, vast
Universe, unlimited *without end*."   Our earthly scientists
with their knowledge of matter have been able to calculate

the age of the Earth, which has existed for several thousand million years.

Yet Zodiac tells us that this planet is of short duration! (as indeed it is, as compared with eternity) and that we were spirit beings before the Earth came into use. We are a long time learning, yet what of the mind of Christ who was even then the Master!

He once told me that He was "In charge of the World." It was suitable for my earthly mind and something I wanted to know, and it also impressed me more than the conventional or "religious" expressions with the same meaning.

During the last war I was taken to the spirit world where there was a group of our soldiers who had just arrived. They were bewildered and helpless with their sudden passing, when in their midst appeared the Master standing head and shoulders above them. They could not see Him and I was staring in amazement, and He quietly said, "I have been with them all the time."

Zodiac once spoke of the "companionship of Christ— that intimate personal companionship which is never absent from you for one second." After I retired I became the secretary of an old people's club. One night I was taken to the spirit world where in a great building Christ was going to manifest to the people. When I went into an anteroom, a man followed me in. At first I sensed the aura of an old-age pensioner—the thoughts, feelings and slower activities—everything.

Then I felt the great emanations of Christ! It was unmistakable and I was dumbfounded. He could see my agitation and smiled and said, "I have dispensed with my beard"—and tried to soothe my agitation with some small talk of everyday things, but I was too excited to take notice. The Modest Gentleman Who bathed the feet of His followers was again trying to veil His Greatness, but I lost the power for consciousness.

"Lo, I am with you always." If it were not so He would not have said it.

The mind of every being has a pulsation and an emission and the Mind of the Master—the Master-mind—

encompasses and contacts all. Some time in eternity we may know the extent of that Mind and perhaps gain a little of that power, although the self-effacing Gentle One said, "Greater things shall ye do."

THE SEARCH FOR A CREATOR

I listened with interest to this recent programme on Radio 4, but like many others, I expect, had misgivings as to the result as the search was through the "Tools of Science."

Science did not seem to know, or have troubled to learn (seek and find) what "Power" it was looking for. Even in the laboratory no scientist has "seen" the actual powers we use on Earth, such as electricity, wind power, steam power, water power (gravity), internal combustion or even his own muscle power—only the *results* are seen.

Yet "God the Creator is Spirit and invisible" has no meaning to the scientist who considered "God" as an unnecessary concept." The astronomer who stood in awe at the "million million galaxies" which he seemed to consider an accidental phenomenon, need not look further than his own doorstep, where there is a speck of dust whose atoms are continually active through an invisible power causing the electrons to encircle the central core.

A telephone caller to the studio, mindful of the scientists' theory of evolution, asked how a sightless creature could develop such a wonderful and delicate organ as an eye.

The scientist's reply was: "By desire."

This made me think of that wonderful creature (as all living things are) which defends itself and obtains its prey simply by thought! It is the electric eel, and one tested in an aquarium registered 650 volts on a voltmeter. Biologists say that it has cells which store the electricity, and which is discharged at will. It must be a knowing creature, as it decided to have its cells "in series" and not "parallel" so as to deliver the maximum voltage!

The invisible powers I mentioned that we use on earth

have been studied and so we now have data, text-books or laws on electricity, steam, etc., and we know and get the results.

There are also laws, spiritual laws of God the Creator, and these were taught in simple form for His generation by Jesus. He showed results even in this material world.

The principal law He taught and lived was to forget "self" and to act, think and speak for the welfare of others, and to be thankful for the Power that gave us life to do so.

He made it clear that an affectation of "holiness" was futile and one *must* be genuine, for we are part of the Power, as even the Power in Him. In my out-of-the-body visits to the spirit world, the direct effect of the laws that Jesus taught are clearly seen in all states.

I also had the impression through many incidents that everything there had a relation to tremendously high-frequency in the electro-magnetic field, and indeed the effect of vibrations is taught in the lectures there. Earth too has its vibrations, as every atom has its pulsation, and we are inured to our particular location or environment.

My eldest brother lived most of his long life in Canada, and when he passed over he went to the Canadian part of the spirit world, his usual country. When I was taken to see him in the spirit world his first question was, "Why can't they see us on earth?" (Oh dear! and I *had* sent him a copy of my book!)

I have been taken to the lower, intermediate, and better states in spirit, and I have always noticed that all are in states according to his or her own inner thoughts and acts, and there are no privileged ones. What law could be more just than that? But the laws of spirit are vast and the progressed ones are continually learning them, which brings them happiness, beauty and beautiful surroundings—they are "in tune" They reason that such perfect laws could not result from accident or chaos, and they have heartfelt thanks and love (worship) for their Creator, and this love is at once returned more fully. (Another spirit law.)

What a difference it would make to this troubled world if all had a change of heart and lived according to the simple teaching of the Master.

THE MIND OF A CHILD

Not long ago I read of the sayings of young children who had been invited to talk about their interests, ideas and their family life. As can be imagined, they were often outspoken, naive and uninhibited, as they had not learnt to be disingenuous, and a domestic upset can have a very sad effect.

One little boy said: "My mummy went away although I loved her." The forlorn loneliness and yearning of a little mind could only express it in such a way, and those who remember their childhood know the heights of happiness and depths of despair a child's mind can reach. Although I am 75, I still remember some fairy tale books I used to read. They were rather grubby little books through much handling, and were called, I think, *Tales For Little People,* and I used to exchange them with another little boy. They were our treasures and created an inward happiness, as the authoress had a wonderful way of describing the flowers, woods, fairy dells, sunny green swards, etc., which delighted us.

My youngest daughter, Eileen, was a happy child. When her mother passed over she readily took to my aunt, who loved children and had come to look after my two daughters.

Once, when she was out shopping with my aunt, my elder daughter came to me and said, "Come and see something" and led me out to our little garden. She pointed to a tulip and inside I found a tiny folded note with Eileen's quaint lettering which said, "Dear fairy, I love you." I said to my daughter, "We must leave something," and remembered I had a tiny silver bell, a bracelet charm, that Eileen had never seen, and left it in the tulip. Later in the day, Eileen came to us happy and excited and with the bell, told us about her letter to the fairies. We told her how lucky she was and Eileen tripped happily back to the garden to "dream dreams."

Eileen was 20 when she passed to the Spirit World in a motor accident. About three years later she told me that she had seen the so-called wee folk or fairies and said they are as gossamer as a spider's web, and seemed to be yet another vibration of the Spirit life. They are devoted to flowers and a flower trodden underfoot is a tragedy to them. She thought it strange how folk-lore and fairy tales have an element of truth.

I have seen her many times in the Spirit World. . . . "Thanks for everything, dad." And I thank God I have not lost my daughter.

GOD'S GREATEST LAW

("Love" is the key that opens all doors in spirit. The Master taught it, and Zodiac always brought it to the fore. These simple creatures, the rabbits, repaid a "love-thought" many times over.)

In my book I referred briefly to an experience I had during astral projection to the Spirit World, and would like to relate it more fully. I was with a spirit friend and we were sitting on the lawn of his spirit home. There were some rabbits playing on the lawn and as we were talking, one of them came close to me and I stroked it. To my surprise all the other rabbits, about 20 of them, ran to me and almost overwhelmed me. They were clambering on my chest with ears back and noses nestling under my chin, all wanting to be caressed, and I was laughing and trying to touch each one. My spirit friend was amused at my surprise and I realised that my friendliness to one rabbit had radiated a thought of love which the other rabbits had sensed. Love from an animal in spirit can be actually felt and gives one a feeling of happiness. When I see people who have a kindly thought for them, I often think of their pleasant surprise later, when they find that their kindness is returned "in full measure and brimming over." Those who kill or wound, not for necessity, but for some strange pleasure, or personal pride of prowess, will, notwithstanding their good points, have the memory of something they fervently wish had never happened. How long does memory last? "Zodiac" has often spoken of his memory of the times and conditions on earth when the Master was teaching, and I once saw an advanced spirit teacher who

said he was born before the Pharaohs.   After 5,000 years
or more, he still had knowledge of his earth life!

Thought is the primary activating essence of everything,
so let us "think" how fortunate we are to have the God-
given gifts of Life, Thought and Memory.   We have to
remember that everything has a rhythmic vibration of
different frequencies, and this also relates to thought.
Thought is an activated vibration, and as thoughts vary, so
do the frequencies.   All thought is impressed upon and
retained by the spirit body.   (Something like the invisible
electron pattern impressed on the tape of a tape-recorder.)

Our collection of thoughts is not a confused jumble, as
each theme has its own frequency and stands apart.   If one
should be asked about something concerning one's schooldays, the detecting brain cells search on *that* frequency for
the answer.

Let us remember this gift of God and dwell on it, for
we each have within us all our past.   All that we have
experienced; incidents, sights, sounds, odours, tastes and
even the clothes worn, all with their own frequency.

Rise up! all ye that bow down to the Moloch
Computer.

Rise up! for you yourself are more wonderful than a
million false Gods.   You are a small portion of God with
inherited gifts.   Thought created—you can create thought
and retain, and remember.   (Your Mum is even better, *she*
can remember *all* the birthdays!)

THAT "KINGDOM"

(The Apostle Andrew.)   "Come child, I would teach
of future things tonight, carry thy mind to scientific
knowledge of today on earth.   Already much is known of
the principles of etheric life, yet none have grasped the
patent fact that this is so.   They still rely upon the
instruments of mental ingenuity, not realizing the import
of that which they now can see. . . . Seest thou how these
experiments with the inner substance of matter lead
inevitably to the discovery of another law of life than that
which forms the outward physical world?   The outer world

is formed of these invisible particles only and of *naught else* but these. . . . Seest thou a parallel in this to the realms of the invisible world of spirit?"

> *From "The Coming Light," by R. M. T.*
> *(Skeffington & Son Ltd.)*

*   *   *   *

(From the Daily Telegraph.)

Daily Telegraph Staff Correspondent,
New York, Sunday.

"An international group of physicists said to-day that there was strong evidence to support one of the most bizarre theories of life: That somewhere there exists an 'anti-world' or even an 'anti-universe.' Dr. Lederman and his associates were the discoverers of the anti-deuteron, the first complex atomic nucleus of anti-matter to be found. Since the anti-deuteron can exist, there is reason to believe that very complex atoms, molecules and even planets of anti-matter can exist also. It is no longer possible to question the basic physics parts of the cosmological conception of a literal anti-world populated by stars and planets and made-up of atoms of anti-matter. Dr. Lederman said: "It is not possible now to disprove the grand speculation that these anti-worlds could be populated by thinking creatures."

*   *   *   *

(Again, to quote the Apostle Andrew.)

"Go forward, men of science, plodding your careful way; soon breaks the light upon your past endeavours showing the goal they tend to, showing the great purpose of your painful toil. Christ gives the strength which fills your minds with love of truth and bids you ever seek until you find and, finding, give salvation to your race."

*   *   *   *

(And to quote the unnamed scribe mentioned in St. Mark's Gospel—12, 28-34—who spoke through Miss Winifred Moyes from 1921 and onward through the war years, the well-loved "Zodiac.")

"There is nothing in physical life which has not its spiritual counterpart in the Realms of Light."

*   *   *   *

As a "thinking creature" who has many times by astral projection visited the spirit states surrounding this world, I would also like to add my humble testimony that I, too, have found this so in the first planes of spirit. It would help us to understand many things if we remember that everything, solid, liquid or gas, has a pulsation or vibration. This is because of the ever-active atomic structure, and it is our God-given "Life" and awareness that is able to differentiate the frequency of pulsaions when we are tasting, smelling, seeing, etc., and so we are able to identify that sensation. I told in a previous article how the free particles (electrical and non-physical) of all atoms gravitated to the magnetic belt surrounding the earth and retained the structure and vibration of their earthly forms. The spirit replicas of earthly things can often be identified, as the spirit body is very sensitive, especially the psychometric faculties. In one spirit state I touched a gun-carriage, a spirit relic of Cromwell's time, and experienced the dreadful feelings of that civil war. In a brighter plane I casually opened a *spirit made* book on Gardens and Homes in spirit and was at once enveloped in the love and friendliness of the author, the welcome of his home, and the beauty of his lawns and gardens. This is one of the many happy surprises in the bright planes. All space is saturated with elementary particles, and in making a spirit object, the concentrated positive thought attracts these negative particles and forms the object thought of, according to the ability of the Spirit Mind.

THE IMPLICATIONS OF ASTRAL PROJECTION

(A letter in the Quarterly Review (March 1965) of The Churches' Fellowship for Psychical & Spiritual Studies.)

Dear Sir,

"Science observes phenomena, discerns conditions, classifies facts, draws inferences, and finally states a theory."

Those who have read Dr. Robert Crookall's books will have noticed that he has carried this out to a remarkable degree.

I have experienced conscious astral projection during the past 28 years, and when Dr. Crookall wrote to me some years ago, I hoped that his investigations and studies would be published as this faculty is not generally known. The outcome—his book, "The Study and Practice of Astral Projection" with 160 case histories, and his masterly summing-up was perhaps a surprise to many.

What does it all amount to? Just further evidence that we *are* indestructable. That we *do* have a spiritual counterpart of the physical body which is ready to be detached at any time. It is quite clear that Jesus, the Master of spiritual knowledge, knew this and spoke of this priceless heritage. To Him, it was such a forthright fact that He spoke of it in compassion for His fellow sufferers even while undergoing the Roman torture of crucifixion, then later proved his survival.

What is this spiritual counterpart of the physical body, and why is it indestructable? We may consider it as a collection of the finer electric particles (electrons in the wider meaning) kept together in magnetic cohesion by the wonderful spark of life given to every living entity.

It encompasses and permeates the physical body and is a parallelism of the nuclear physicists' theory that certain atomic particles have a particle-counterpart—the "mirror image" theory. The spirit body therefore is in a continuous electrical activity in a myriad of wave-forms through the body functions and ever-changing thoughts and awareness. The slower and more physical wave-forms can be recorded on the electro-encephalograph.

As in other forms of electrical activity (transformers, dynamos, etc.) the spirit body has an emission or field surrounding it, forming a nimbus or aura, and seen spiritually has a bluish tint. This aura is very sensitive and forms part of one's awarenes. On one occasion during astral projection, when I was with some spirit friends, someone aproached me from behind and put their arms around me. I at once *knew* it was my wife—*and* also the dress she was wearing. When I turned I found my impression was correct. Jesus through His great spirituality was able, even in a crowd, to sense that a woman had touched his gown. Her thoughts (an electric emission) and touch (contact of personal wave-form) was sensed by his great aura.

What of His teachings?

Those who have read my book on astral projection "Excursions to the Spirit World" (C.F.P.S.S. *Quarterly Review*, March 1962) will have noticed that the "sowing and reaping" of which Jesus spoke is quite apparent in the people and the different states they inhabit in spirit, for the sheep *are* separated from the goats. The thoughts during the earthly life of a person, being a wave-form, are impressed on the spirit body. This is the mechanics of memory, which has been so elusive to the brain specialist and will never be found in the medical sense.

A person during earth life has an enormous collection of different thoughts (different wave-forms) yet the sum total has an average—which is the spiritual status *and* locality of that person on entry into spirit life.

Yours faithfully,

F. C. SCULTHORP.

PSYCHOMETRY AND ITS SIGNIFICANCE

Many have had proof of this particular gift that some mediums possess in the sensing of events in a person's life, interests, occupations, etc., simply by holding an article belonging to that person.

At a small church I used to attend, a demonstration of psychometry was to be held and members were asked to bring a flower or even a sprig from a privet hedge. The medium preferred this, as a plant has not had the various contacts that some articles may have had, and a well-defined demonstration was given.

Psychometry is just as wonderful as other spirit laws, as it concerns the animate, the vital principle or soul of the personality. To think that a flower held for a short time could be impressed (or magnetised as some say) by the owner's memory of past years is beyond all earthly knowledge or reasoning. Some who are considered to have an abundance of that mental capacity have brushed it aside as "thought reading" and have ignored the invitation to try it by post, as many have done.

"Memory" is incorporated in the whole of the physical body and spirit body within; the latter being composed of replica particles of every atom of the physical body.

Thought is electrical activity and has an electron pattern and frequency which is retained by the two bodies, physical and spiritual. The tape-recorder that impresses an electron pattern on the ferrous tape is an analogy, except that the living entity's thoughts have a frequency that is millions plus that of our earthly instruments, and can impress itself on most things.

This is also the reason why telepathic thought with its small "energy" can overcome distance by its tremendously high-frequency of vibration.

Some who practise psychometry not only receive impressions but have pictures, scenes, music and oft-repeated names in that person's memory. Psychometry and telepathy are only two of the spiritual gifts we all have dormant within us, and during astral projection to the spirit world I have found them surprising at first, but quite easy and natural. Other gifts follow and are noticed when the occasion occurs.

One I experienced was the split-second awareness that the spirit body has and was a happy surprise. My spirit teacher had taken me to a social party in the spirit world, and I was talking to a pretty little child when two arms hugged me from behind. Immediately I mentally saw my wife and the dress she wore. When I turned—it *was* my wife and that same dress!

It was another happy meeting, and I have often thought of that faculty of the spirit body of seeing *backwards*.

In the spirit body the surrounding aura is also part of the mind and personal awareness, and when it is entered even from behind, it is registered in a very wonderful way.

On earth the great spiritual aura of Jesus registered the intention and deliberate touch of His garment by someone and He remarked on it.

CLOSING NOTE

I hope this little book has interested you. If so, it will please your gentle spirit helper, who tries to lead your thoughts. He/She has always watched over you.

If you are lonely, perhaps an experience that happened after my daughter Eileen passed over will interest you.

It was evening and I had closed my shop and was sitting alone in my armchair in the living room. It was quiet—too quiet and I felt lonely, and I sank into the state in which I became alert and aware in my spirit body. I could hear music and the happy laughter of many people coming from the sitting-room upstairs, just like the parties we used to have when my wife was on earth. I felt that the house was full of our friends and relatives.

Presently, Eileen came tripping through the room I was sitting in. She was smiling happily and had an ice-cream cornet in one hand and a banana in the other—a lick and a bite—the favourite "treat" of her schooldays. She went into the garden and I looked in the kitchen, and on the "Ascot" heater over the sink there was a crude notice hanging—"to the band"—and an arrow pointing to the garden. (I sensed it was Eileen's handiwork.) In my garden there was a heap of coal, the overflow from the small bunker, and when I went out there was a group of bandsmen with instruments and their uniforms, taking their ease—on the heap of coals!

The comic tableau of those splendid uniforms and the laughing bandsmen who took part, and their spiritual immunity from the dust and grime of earthly coal, was too funny to last. I was drawn back to my physical body in the armchair, a bit dazed, but still full of the "party spirit," and my loneliness dispelled. I mentally blessed my daughter and those with her. She used to work with me in my shop, and had a lively sense of humour.—F. C. S.

A Treatise on

THE ELECTRO-MAGNETIC BASIS OF THE SPIRIT BODY AND ITS FACULTIES

Lessons and impressions received during conscious astral projections and through clairvoyance.

By

FREDERICK C. SCULTHORP

CONTENTS

INTRODUCTION

1. During 28 years of personal experience of astral projection and clairvoyance I have learned that all parapsychological manifestations are electro-magnetic in origin. I have been to the spirit realms many times and have for a long time held the theories explained in this treatise. Some of the theories were formed through a repetition of the experiences, and many of these experiences are related in my book *Excursions to the Spirit World* (Almorris Press Ltd., London). In the book I have simply given causes and effects, as the deeper issues of psychic science would not interest, or perhaps would not be understood by the average reader.

2. However, with the continual advance of science, even the reader of the daily paper must be impressed by the references to nuclear physics and radiation. The emanations received from a satellite that has long left earth, or from the far away nebula, gives some idea of the effect of wave-forms and the apparatus needed. Yet the living entity far outshines anything in this direction, for no laboratory apparatus can detect and separate all the evanescent wave-forms which constitute the different tastes and odours we experience.

3. Fine and delicate as these senses are, they are gross and earthly compared with the much higher rate of wave-form of spirit, and if we keep this in mind, some of the causes and effects in the spirit hypothesis will be understood.

The Spirit Body

4. The spirit body encompasses and permeates the physical body and is a replica of the atoms forming that body. This replica consists of the finer electric particles (or electrons in the wider sense) of the parent atoms and therefore assumes that pattern. Although associated with

the parent atoms, these particles are also in magnetic cohesion actuated by a superior life-force of the living entity. The life-force causing the magnetic cohesion of the particles forming the physical counterpart also forms a spirit body that is indestructible.

5. During astral projection to the lower and intermediate planes, I am exactly the same as on earth. After many journeys the likeness being similar, I habitually thought of myself as being the double in all respects of my physical state. I now associate this with the nuclear physicists' theory that certain atomic particles have a particle-counterpart. On one occasion during astral projection, I looked down on my clothes and was surprised to see that my trousers had a faint white stain on them, the same as on earth, where I had dropped some tooth-paste. This seems to be a clear implication of the "mirror image" as even the particle-counterparts of the faint stain were there.

6. There is, of course, a cohesion of the particles forming the spirit replica of an earthly object, but this can be dispersed. The spirit body cannot be dispersed and is indestructible.

7. On entry to spirit life it sometimes happens that the particle-counterpart of the physical body persists for a time, as in the case of a cripple. There is no pain, as that particular necessity of the nervous system in the physical body has finished, but an adjustment is soon made with the help of spirit experts in these cases. I once saw a small child who was a hunchback and had not become conscious to spirit life.

The Electrical Properties of the Spirit Body

8. Through the body functions (heart action, etc.) and ever-changing thoughts and awareness, the spirit body is in continuous electrical activity in a myriad of wave-forms. The *slower* of these can be recorded on the electro-encephalograph. As in other forms of electrical activity, the spirit body has an emission or field surrounding it, forming a nimbus or aura, and seen spiritually generally has a bluish tint. This aura is very sensitive and forms part of one's awareness, particularly when in contact with other

auras, and in certain conditions, contact with inanimate objects.

9. The "electrical" properties of the spirit body are very apparent at times. During a projection I once grasped the hands of a spirit, and he at once fell down as if unconscious.

10. Through the contrast with the duller conditions, the aura of an advanced spirit is easily seen if he visits a lower plane.

11. I once heard insults shouted to one of these by a low spirit. At a distance of about 20 yards he subdued his aggressor by an extrusion of his powers, and the man sank to the ground as if all his strength had gone.

12. In my very first projection in 1936 I learned something about the aura. It was during the night and I was taken only a short distance. I found myself standing behind a table in front of which a line of young men were passing and smiling towards me. They all appeared to be about 23 years of age and dressed in blue. They had beautiful eyes and features, and then I noticed that they were wearing ordinary clothes and that the blue was a haze surrounding each one.

13. Inwardly I was excited, but my inquisitiveness came to the fore and not knowing much about spirit life then, I wondered if now being a spirit myself, they would feel "solid" to me. I could hardly go to one of these splendid-looking young men and deliberately touch him. One of them was standing beside me at the table, and I thought up the wonderful idea of passing behind him in a casual manner, at the same time saying, "Excuse me" and touching him as I passed. This I did, but directly I touched him he grasped my hands with a laugh. I had to laugh too as I was at once aware that he knew of my intentions, and I also *knew* that he knew. In the mingling of auras, all thoughts are known, and spirit bodies on the same wave-length are as solids to each other.

14. On another occasion during a projection when I was with some spirit friends, someone approached me from behind and embraced me. I at once *knew* it was my wife who had passed over, and *also* the dress she was wearing.

When I turned I found my impression was correct. It is recorded in the Bible that even in a crowd, Jesus knew that somebody had touched his gown and sensed the personality of a woman.

15. I have had many experiences during projection in the contact of auras, and the past lives of some individuals are very strongly impressed on the spirit body, which in turn impregnates the zone or aura surrounding them. I once contacted a very cheerful and friendly looking man who had the strongest personality that I had ever met in the spirit state. He rode the lead horse of a gun-carriage in Cromwell's Army during the Civil War in England about the year 1642, and standing within his aura I *saw* his life, the most prominent impressions being his war experiences. His personality was the toughest I had ever sensed, and together with the harshness of that historic period, was a shock to my feelings. Like a film I saw his part in the many battles, skirmishes and incidents of gallantry and recklessness which were so vivid that they seemed to be actually happening. It is surprising how the spirit body can hold such strong impressions of incidents that happened 300 years ago.

The Controlling Influence of the Life-force

16. The life-force and awareness of the living entity has directive powers over the electrical properties of the spirit body. Thought causes a movement of electrons and therefore a wave-form. All thoughts throughout life (physical and after) form a *continuous* magnetically cohesive *chain* of electrons. This chain of electrons (with its myriads of wave-forms) is the life experiences of the living entity and embodies all thoughts, sights, sounds and even wide scenic impressions, as the electrons have no mass. The "chain" of life also automatically records the clothing worn at different periods, by the magnetic impression caused by the emission of the particle-counterparts of the atoms of that cloth.ng.

17. This continuous chain of the individual's past is always on hand and "time" is eliminated, for the past is present, yet there is sequence. When a person thinks of an incident of his past, his thought of that particular incident naturally

has the same wave-rate as the stored magnetic impression, and thus this particular "memory" is contacted. This is the mechanics of memory and it will never be "isolated" by the brain specialist, as it is, together with other thoughts, on the higher spiritual wave-rate and makes communication between earthly and spirit minds possible.

Although the spirit body holds all past thoughts by magnetic impressions, they are not a confused jumble but joined and consecutive. One evening, when I was sitting at home and had reached the clairvoyant state, a spirit appeared before me. He was an elderly man and he stepped forward and stood beside me, entering my aura. Immediately his whole life, from birth to physical death, passed before me like a cine film. It was a full life with many outstanding incidents, and it lasted about *one second*. I tried to contemplate some of the incidents of his life, but the whole thought left me in a flash. Being in a clairvoyant state I was able to note his spiritual record with my spiritual senses, *but* I tried to contemplate with my physical mentality, which is a million times slower. However, I was able to remember that the spiritual thought record of the man was in sequence and continuous like a chain.

18. At one period during my experiences in astral projection, I used to be taken to lectures on one of the spirit planes. On one occasion as I was entering the lecture room I momentarily had a flash-back or recap of the three previous lectures. It was quite instantaneous, yet they were in their entirety and in sequence, which is very helpful as in spirit one has to know certain things to understand others. This is another instance of the chain-like sequence of stored memory. These experiences also show the electric-like speed of the spirit mind.

19. In amnesia through shock of accident, there is a complete blank in the line of memory, and sometimes the shock even erases the memory of happenings for a period *before* the accident. I believe that a physical shock causes a psychic and electric blast or upheaval disturbing even the magnetic impression recorded *before* the accident.

20. The following experience gives that impression. When I was a shopkeeper I used to sit in a back room after lunch

to get in the clairvoyant state. The armchair I sat on backed on to the shop and main road. One day when I was sitting in this state, which is very sensitive, I suddenly felt a terrific blast like an explosion hit me from behind—yet I knew there was no physical noise. I had never experienced this before. A minute later my assistant hurried through the room saying, "A girl has just fallen off her bicycle. She is all right, but I'll get her a glass of water." When my assistant came back later I asked her what happened. She said a girl and her friend were cycling, their handlebars locked, and the girl fell on her hands and knees with an awful smack and was dazed. I connect the spiritual "blast" I received with the shock the girl's psychic senses had received, radiating a shock-wave.

21. One afternoon a clairvoyant friend of mine, who is very sensitive, entered my shop looking worried. She had just got off a bus and said that when the bus was passing a certain point she felt shocked, as if something dreadful had happened. She looked through the window of the bus and could see nothing unusual, but she was sure something had happened. When the local paper was published, we read that there was a road accident at that spot on that afternoon, and a person taken to hospital. My friend said that she had experienced this before, and declared that an accident leaves a "psychic impression" in the vicinity for a period.

22. Adopting the clothing of any period of their past earth life is easy to spirits who know how. It is done by thinking back to that period where the electrons forming that clothing are impressed on the chain of memory. On one occasion, during a projection, my spirit teacher made me adopt the army uniform I wore in the first world war. The reason for this was that he was going to take me on a visit to a very low plane, which has a harsh effect on the spirit body, and in adopting the war period clothing I also took on my tougher nature of that period.

23. I once saw an advanced spirit on a lower plane, where he had come to teach. He would have been quite invisible to the people on the lower plane, but in adopting his earthly clothing he took on denser particles with a slower wave-rate. He said he was born before the Pharoahs and was wearing

a kind of Arab gown. Thinking back 50 centuries or more is quite a feat, but the massless indestructible electrons were still there.

24. Those who have studied psychic science will know that in the spirit state, objects can be created by thought. This is another instance of the ability of the spirit body to use its inherent electrical powers. All space is densely saturated with free electrons (electrical particles with their particular properties). This is now being recognized by atomic physicists. A thought which is positive, directive and electrical, at once brings these negative particles rushing together in magnetic cohesion, thus forming the object thought of. According to the strength and degree of the thought, so is the object temporary or more lasting. This is a natural and intrinsic power of the spirit body, as the following incident will show.

25. During a projection I watched a man who had only recently entered spirit life, and was becoming conscious. He was a neatly dressed man, and as his eyes gradually opened, the complete keyboard of an organ appeared above him and then dissolved. I sensed that he played the organ and that it was his uppermost interest. It seems impossible that a half-conscious man can "make" an organ keyboard with its many keys, stops, etc. But a perfect picture of his keyboard was impressed on his chain of memory and his thought brought the particles rushing together to form the perfect replica. The thought and the cohesive power being weak, the structure was temporary.

Wave-lengths

26. As the spirit body contains all life's thoughts, and thoughts differ, so do the wave-rates. There is, however, a sum total of these wave-rates—and an *average rate*. This average is the personal "wave-length" of the individual. As no two people can possibly have a collection of thoughts exactly the same wave-length, every individual is unique. This is why telepathy has occurred in physical life, and is very easy in spirit life. This wave-length also decides the state and spiritual status on entry into spirit life.

27. The idea of a personal wave-length for each of us

sounds fantastic considering the millions it involves, but even the slower physical senses can do fantastic things. Light rays have the rate of many millions, and different colours have different frequencies, yet the eyes automatically register these differences and we see the colours. Light rays are considered to be an electro-magnetic disturbance, and living entities have a "built-in" process for "detecting" the difference in the wave-rates, *and* we unconsciously and naturally do it.

28. There are several reasons and experiences for my theory of a personal wave-length.

29. One day I was leaning on my shop counter idly watching the passing traffic, when I had an impression that my sister-in-law was coming. The impression of her personality and the thought that she was coming was so strong that I made a note of the time. Half-an-hour later my sister-in-law walked into my shop and said, "Did you get anything?" Naturally we were both pleased at the result of her experiment, and I asked her how did she do it?

30. She said, "I tried to visualize myself as standing before you and saying, 'I am coming,' and I repeated this several times before leavng the house and taking the bus."

My sister-in-law's place was half-an-hour's bus ride from my shop. It will be noticed that I was in a *natural* receptive state.

The experiment was not suggested between us. My sister-in-law usually visited us on Sundays, and not a week-day when the experiment was tried. We lived in Greater London and her telepathic thought reached the *right person* among eight million people. When she radiated her message she thought of my personality (an automatic tuning-in to my wave-length)—her radiated thought also carried her personality (wave-length) which I received. (In distant telepathy, therefore, the personality must be known between two in the physical body.)

31. My wife had passed over when I started astral projection in 1936, and naturally my greatest desire was to meet her. On my fourth projection I landed in a country lane in one of the spirit planes, and knowing the possibilities

of telepathy I simply thought of her and said, "Come." After a short pause my wife suddenly appeared about 10 yards away down the lane, and walked towards me. We did *not* ponder over the mechanics of telepathy—we had other emotions. After many experiences, I am still surprised that it is so natural and easy in the spirit state; telepathy from my wife sounds as if she is standing beside me and I can recognize her voice.

32. The trouble with newcomers in spirit is not how to use telepathy, but how to prevent it, as at short distances one does not have to know the person thought of.

33. On one occasion my wife took me to a concert on her plane. One of the turns was a man singer, and I thought he was overdoing his gestures. Twice I thought this, and at the end of his song the man came to the edge of the stage and gave me a nasty look. We hurriedly left the hall and I realized that he had received my thoughts.

34. On another occasion I was walking with my wife in a park in her particular state, and two women passed us. When they were some distance away I felt a strange connection with them, and then realized that they were talking about us. The concluding sentence of one woman was, "Oh yes, she is looking after her husband and two children on earth." (Myself and my two daughters.)

35. Pleasant thoughts are appreciated. On one projection to an institution I passed the open door of a room where a lecture was being given. Having a side-face view of the lecturer, I was surprised to see that he was once an officer in my unit in the 1914 war. I was pleased to see by his appearance (fine features, colouring and a certain brightness) that his spiritual status was advanced. He received my thoughts, and turned and smiled towards me.

36. When I meet my wife she sometimes has one or two small children in her charge. Once I wished quite casually that one would sit by my side at a table. The child at once came and sat beside me.

37. It will, therefore, be seen that the emission of thought from the spirit body is a natural faculty and at once noticed in the spirit state, but when conjoined with a physical body

these senses are damped. However, that it still takes place is proved by the evidence that a thought from one on earth reaches one in the spirit state, and by the cases of proved telepathy between two in the physical body.

38. The greater power of collective thought may have some effect on the physical senses, and may be associated with mob violence, revivalist meetings, or theatre fire panic even when there is no sign of immediate danger.

39. In my personal experience of telepathy on earth, I mentioned my *natural* receptive state. In experimental telepathy the receiver generally concentrates on being receptive. This is mental activity and the receptive state only arrives when the concentration tires and the mind is quiescent. The sender who *should* concentrate on the emitted thought, unfortunately, does not know when the receiver has reached a receptive state, so there are not many successes.

40. There has been proof of telepathy between married couples, the most outstanding being the Piddington's, who demonstrated on the radio sometimes 200 miles apart. It perplexed Lord Simon, chairman of the British Broadcasting Corporation, and his radio engineer, as unlike the music hall act no code could be used as they were not allowed radio contact.

41. In Russia there has been successful telepathy by a suitable subject under hypnosis. They have also found that the personality must be known, which agrees with my theory that each of us has a personal wave-length.

42. They also state that they have enclosed their subject in a metal screen, and telepathy still occurs; therefore it has had no connection with electro-magnetic waves. I consider that it is a much faster rate of electro-magnetic waves, as psychic research has established that lightning-storms also affect spirit communication, as well as radio and other forms of electro-magnetic waves.

43. If we consider the range between low-frequency and ultra-high-frequency, and *then* the enormous leap to the millions plus rate of the thought emission, we can understand why the usual screening method would be no

more effective than using a voltmeter instead of the electro-encephalograph for recording the electrical changes connected with the thought impulses.

44. As thought impulses affect an apparatus, we know that there is electrical activity. The established scientific facts that magnetism is inseparably connected with electricity, and that a flow will certainly cause an electro-magnetic field (aura), are well known. Also that disturbances in the electrical and magnetic conditions at one place can be propagated to another place through empty space. (Maxwell equations.)

45. As we now know of these disturbances by thought, there is no reason why a like organism should not be affected through space with the same disturbances, which forms the thought contact.

46. The stored chain of memory held by the spirit body mentioned in para. 16, with its many different thoughts and their myriads of wave-rates, has a certain quality taken as a whole. They are a collection of high, medium and low thoughts, and that also refers literally to the wave-rates of these thoughts. The high wave-rates are associated with unselfish love or outward (and mental) amenity in its many forms. The medium wave-rates would be the generalities of life, and the low concern the many forms of selfishness and unconcern for others. Naturally, there must be thought before the act, but thought without the act is still impressed.

47. The average wave-rate of all these thoughts is the nature or character of the person, and we see examples all around us. It is also the wave-length of the person. Unlike the crude wave-length of radio, it has the subtlety of spirit, and has a number of infinitesimal wave-lengths in the unification composing and forming that wave-length. On entry into spirit life, the spirit body gravitates to its corresponding wave-length in the spirit realms.

48. It is known that there is a magnetic belt surrounding the earth. It is also known that gravitation has no effect on free particles. The magnetic belt *has* an attraction for the particles saturating space, and according to their particular qualities, so *that* magnetic attraction operates. There is a natural grading of these particles owing to their particular

qualities; the slower and denser being close to earth, then the less dense, and so on outwards to the ever finer particles with their higher wave-rate.

49. Experiences in astral projection seem to agree with this. The various degrees of low states have a varying degree of light owing to the slower wave-rate of the particles, the lowest states almost resembling twilight. Going up the scale, so the states get brighter. The highest state I went to was brilliant, like noon in the tropics. The nature of the inhabitants agrees with the varying degrees of states. The lowest contain the aggressive, the vicious and the many other different kinds of low mentality. In the higher states, friendliness is noticeable everywhere. I therefore take it that low thoughts cause the spirit body to have a low wave-length, and the high thoughts a high one, and I have never seen a spirit whose nature did not agree with the locality.

50. On a low state I tried levitation and found it very difficult. It needed a great effort of will to rise as high as the first floor of a house, and I could not hold it. On a high plane it was extremely easy and I could rise and travel as I wished. My spirit body seemed very light, and I had the idea that it was through the shedding of particles.

Psychometry

51. The storing of all life's incidents in the spirit body, the wave-forms of which are continually in the aura, also has the effect of impressing these wave-forms on some articles carried by the individual. They can also impregnate the house and furniture.

52. One of the most apparent proofs that the laws of electro-magnetism also relate to the spirit body is seen in psychometry. Many sensitives find that their easiest psychic faculty is the sensing of impressions of the life of the owner of an article. The article having been in proximity with the owner's aura has therefore been within the magnetic field containing the owner's electrical thought patterns. These can even be impressed on the owner's furniture and house.

53. "Yram," the French astral projectionist, wished to go

to a friend who had gone to live in another district. Having previously given a piece of furniture to this friend, he concentrated on it for his personal impressions, and arrived at the new home.

54. As there are no signposts in space, this is also a spirit's method of returning to his previous home on earth.

Emission of Radiation

55. Another of the powers which the spirit body possesses is the ability to project a ray or surge of the electrical forces in any desired direction. It can also send out a more subtle and far-reaching radiation in all directions, like a radio transmitting station.

56. During projection I have experienced this ability of the spirit body to emit some part of its electrical power. This is quite automatic and natural, and needs no special effort of thought. If I have been interested in a person who is some distance away, the mere *desire* to see more clearly seems to send a surge of my personality so close that I can even see the colour of the eyes, yet I do not move from the spot.

57. On one occasion my spirit teacher enabled me to experience this on a higher plane. I was taken to the side of a mountain overlooking a large plain. Some distance away I could see two people who were mere specks. As I got interested in them, I began to see that they were seated side by side and were dressed as Hindus. My interest increased, and so did my spiritual contact, and I saw the spot between the eyes affected by some Indian women. I also contacted their personalities and *knew* they were man and wife ,and also that they had been in the spirit realms for a long time yet I did not move from my spot on the side of the mountain.

58. I believe that this has a connection with "travelling clairvoyance"—the ability of a sensitive to describe accurately distant buildings or localities.

59. It is obvious that the spirit body sends out a radiating thought in all directions like a transmitting station, because in distant telepathy the sender does not know the direction of the receiver, and this can be seen in other examples.

60. Animals use their senses more than intellect or reasoning power, and the homing abilities of pigeons and other domestic animals have an explanation. The pigeon on release naturally thinks of "home" and "where" and sends out a radiating thought and contacts its house like the projectionist in para. 53. Some pigeon fanciers say that they use landmarks, but this could not be so as they have been released over the Atlantic.

61. One pigeon expert related the following, which he thought was strange:—

A man in London bought a pigeon from a fancier in the Midlands. As is usual, he kept it in for a period to get used to the pigeon loft. However, when he released it, the pigeon did not return. He wrote to the previous owner, who replied that the pigeon had returned to him. But he said that he was now living in *Wales,* where he had taken the same pigeon loft. The pigeon had not returned to the old locality, but to its *familiar loft.*

62. It was reported that when pigeons were released near a powerful transmitting station in Canada, they lost their homing instinct. This is another pointer that electromagnetic waves are involved.

63. It will be noticed that homing is not a haphazard wandering with pigeons and other domestic animals, as they take a direct route. It was reported in our national press that a farmer had removed from Devonshire to a farm in Scotland, taking his cat with him. In four weeks the cat returned to its old home, a distance of 300 miles and more.

64. Another item in the press, which was called a mystery, stated: "A cow whose calf was taken and sold in the market got out during the night and found its calf. In *one night* it had found its calf, which was 30 miles away on a farm. At some point it had to cross the river Thames— nobody knows where."

The cow had radiated the anxious thought and contacted the magnetic emissions of a very personal belonging.

65. One mystery was explained to me by my spirit teacher in a novel way. Some few years ago one of our national

daily papers published letters from readers who stated that their dogs knew when they were nearing home. Their wives said that the dogs got excited some little time before their arrival. Some thought the dogs recognized the sound of their car engines, even though they were driving popular makes, and many passed the house.

66. Some time later my cousin and his wife, with their dog, called on me. His wife went out to see the shops, and later in the evening we were talking together in a back room when the dog whimpered and went to the door of the room. My cousin laughed and said the dog knew his wife was coming back. About 20 seconds later the door-bell rang, and it *was* his wife.

67. His wife was not using a car, and I lived in a busy main road; it was Saturday evening and many shoppers were passing, so that the dog could not have recognized footsteps.

68. A few nights later during a projection, my spirit teacher told me to walk towards a solitary house. When it was about 40 yards distant, a constant overall stream of bright sparks or particles issued from my spirit body and entered the house. I approached the side of the house and then the back, and the same thing happened. Like some lessons, it was rather emphasized and the emissions almost looked like incendiary bullets, but I could see his point. We may then take it that, besides the aura, which only extends for inches, there is also another constant emission of a greater extent, and that is what some dogs can sense.

69. As well as the overall electro-magnetic influence of the earth, all localities on earth have their own particular electro-magnetic emanation. As the emanation is from masses, and the composition of masses must differ—even as the atomic composition of two pin-points must differ— so localities have this distinction. It could be seen in the case of the salmon; the living organism, the ova of the salmon, is impressed with the particular emanation of its locality (the same as the personal article in the aura) and later in adult life has a particular attraction to the locality where it was spawned.

70. The electro-magnetic influence of the earth masses has

a correlation in the magnetic belt surrounding the earth, and in psychic research it has been found that spirits go to surroundings and racial influences as experienced on earth. In my projections to the spirit states I have always found this so. This separation of races and the counterparts of their earth localities occurs in the first few states, but on higher planes I have seen other nationalities, as the finer spirit body has more freedom from the earth's magnetic influence. Therefore, a higher spirit can visit lower states, but not vice versa.

The Fine Texture of the Spirit Body

71. During astral projection the spirit body has a finer texture in the higher spirit realms than in the lower.

72. As the different states or planes in the spirit realms have different wave-lengths, during astral projection my spirit body, having its own personal wave-length, did not coincide with all of them. However, my spirit teacher could make it denser or finer, according to the lesson or experience. Sometimes I would be quite invisible to people on a lower state, and when not knowing this, I spoke to them, they look round quite scared. Others would walk through me, but I could feel nothing as our wave-lengths differed, and like the radio wave-lengths, interpenetrated without interference. A lady walked through me when I had projected to a place on earth, and again I felt nothing. Apparently, the spirit body can assume many different densities or conditions, as it is not always affected when contacting the auras of others.

73. On a higher plane, the spirit body feels light and active and there is a continual happy feeling. I associated this with the higher wave-length, but the feeling increases when near any of the inhabitants, as they all emit a feeling of great friendship and I felt as if I knew them all. I believe that transferring all thoughts of self for others has the effect of raising the wave-length of the spirit body, and this is the reason for their higher state in spirit.

74. Travel in the higher states can be very fast, and my spirit teacher once arranged a demonstration. I had projected and was taken to a vast grassy plain and told to

wait. As I looked round expectantly I saw two pin-points of light in the distance. They seemed to get brighter, and then suddenly became two orbs of blue-white light which were travelling towards me at tremendous speed. Before I had time to be startled, they stopped before me and were two young men. They were two of my army companions of the 1914 war. In this higher form of travel the spirit form was not visible to me, and the personality while travelling was like a ball of energy.

75. Like the radio wave-lengths, two different states sometimes interpenetrate and each is invisible and independent of the other. Lessons in the low states can become depressing and once, on my arrival, I expressed dissatisfaction. My spirit teacher at once reduced the density of my spirit body, and the miserable-looking place disappeared and I was standing in the bright countryside, without having moved from the spot.

76. Anger, or even annoyance, has the temporary but immediate effect of lowering the wave-length of the spirit body. Several times during projection my spirit body has been visible to those in the lower states. Some of these have an animosity to an intruder, whom they can recognize. Once, a gang of these people jumped on me and, in my fighting-mad state, my astral cord drew me back to the physical body like an elastic cable, with a curious effect. These people were hanging on to me, and as I entered my physical body there was a bright flash, and they were flung in all directions. It seemed that the re-uniting of my two bodies produced a higher electrical potential which has great repulsive effect. (This repulsion is explained in para. 79.)

77. Many years ago my two young daughters were on holiday at the Isle of Wight, a seaside resort about 90 miles from London. I projected from an armchair and joined them. They were playing with a ball and during the game the elder one accidently hit a lady in the back with it. I felt annoyed over it, and immediately began to recede. I tried to resist it, but it was no use and I was whipped back to my physical body. It seemed to take about three seconds of time. When my daughters returned at the week-end, I

told the elder one what I had seen. She reddened and admitted it; the younger one giggled happily over her big sister's discomfiture at having been "found out."

Some Aspects of Astral Projection

78. The phenomena of astral projection has often been recorded and in quite recent years a scientist has published a book containing 160 case histories. In my own case and a few others the projections have been numerous. Some have perhaps had a single spontaneous experience. Never-the less, the experiences should be made known and any correlation in the phenomena noted and inferences drawn.

79. The repulsive effect between spirit bodies mentioned under para. 76 is explained in the following:—

After having projected many times, I used to wonder why I never accidentally knocked against another person or object, as, when "in tune" with that state, all things feel solid. I could not experiment as that would not be an accident, so my spirit teacher arranged an incident. During a projection I was induced to run round a corner, and unexpectedly ran full tilt into a group of people also about to turn the corner. I felt as if I had hit a soft cushion of air and was diverted round the group. I then knew that spirit bodies were the same "polarity" and therefore repelled. This, of course, would not occur when the mind directs.

80. Sometimes, when arriving on a plane during projection, the surroundings were not very clear to me. Then, on touching some object belonging to that plane, I would become "in tune" and everything became crystal clear. Wondering why standing did not make this connection, I was told that standing was a habit, but a deliberate touch meant thought for that act and therefore made the contact, and I became near the same potential.

Observations on the Electro-magnetic Theory of Parapsychological Phenomena

81. It is an inexorable law that the progeny must bear some resemblance to its progenitors, and we know that this is not by chance; that there must be a cause. We also

know that in psychometry an article is impressed by simply being in the aura of the owner; the embryo of all living things, by their closeness to the parental source must have a complete impression.

An advanced spirit teacher said that he could see the pattern of the oak tree by looking at an acorn.

82. This surrounding electron copy must be the pattern that the ever-multiplying cells of the new growth must follow. Physical mishaps may cause a deviation, but the cells are still attracted to the pattern. In some lower forms of life like the crab, a severed claw will cause a resumption of cell growth until the pattern is once more complete.

This fine web of the electron pattern accompanies all living things, and where the genus and pattern coincide making the strongest outline, the progeny is a copy. The high cheekbones of two Asiatics persist, but an Asiatic and a European pattern almost coincide and there is a modification as the two patterns interweave, and the growing cells follow the strongest coincidence. Medical science has often wondered at the "fault" in nature in giving the male false nipples, but it is the faithful electron pattern of *both* the progenitors which coincide, and later follows the course of one in physical characteristics.

83. Cell growth is not haphazard, otherwise every living thing would have abnormalities. When these do happen, medical science is beginning to trace the physical mishaps connected with the genes and chromosomes. The passing on of the forebear characteristics, whether it is in the acorn or the mushroom spore, must carry a resemblance in the infinitesimal electrons and wave-rates. The swarm of minute newly-hatched spiders, without reasoning power, soon build webs likened to the best civil engineering, yet every web differs according to the supporting points.

84. A further example of electro-magnetic impression by association can be seen in the experiments with the planarium, or flat worm. These experiments by James McConel fascinated the scientific world and were carried further by W. C. Corning and E. R. John at Rochester, New York. These worms contracted when given an electric shock

accompanied with a bright light. After many trials, they contract even when just the light is switched on, thus proving the existence of a memory. The worm, if severed, has the ability to regenerate; the tail will grow a new head, and the head will grow a new tail, and four weeks later there are two fully grown worms. It was found that not only does the head end remember to contract with the light, but the tail with its new head remembers also. The scientific report at the time said that the memory present in the head where the brain is, and also in the tail prior to cutting, is simply explained; the flat worm has a unique nervous system!

85. Such a unique nervous system would not need a centralized brain, when even the memory is in the severed tail.

It is not known by those unacquainted with parapsychology that, although the physical brain is concerned only with physical functions, among the millions of cells there are certain cells whose only physical function is to act as "detectors" (in the radio sense) in picking up the electro-magnetic impressions of thought and memory, the electrical nature of which is proved by the use of the electro-encephalograph. This " thought" is in the whole body and the tail follows the electro-magnetic law as it is in the same "field" of activity.

86. When the new head and brain grows on the severed tail, it is able to detect the magnetic impressions of its previous discomfort. The flat worm is unique in surviving after this severence, but where did it get the pattern for the new head before even the brain formed?—which is another problem for those who study cell growth.

Conclusions

87. The following demonstrable facts all lead to the inevitable conclusion that some form of electro-magnetism is involved in all phenomena associated with the spirit body (whether coexistent with the physical body or after): —

(a) The present day use of the electro-encephalograph proves that there is electrical activity in the brain.

(b) Wherever an electric current flows, there must be a surrounding field or aura.

(c) This aura is seen by sensitives around the physical body and around disembodied spirits.

(d) Objects within the scope of this field can be impressed with its characteristic pattern of wave-forms, just as a recording tape is impressed with a pattern of sound waves. (The millions plus higher rate of the living mind can impress most substances.)

(e) The impression of thoughts of the owner on a personal article can be demonstrated by psychometry.

(f) Electro-magnetic waves cannot be disassociated from the electro-magnetic qualities of the spirit body. That these can be radiated by conscious thought or by natural desire has been proved beyond doubt.

(g) Lightning-storms affect both radio communication and spirit communication, proving that each is a system of electro-magnetic waves.

88. In addition, my experiences of astral projection have furnished me with innumerable proofs, which cannot be demonstrated, that the "life-force" is imbued with electro-magnetic qualities; I have related a few examples.

89. In astral projection, I consider the two separate bodies to be joined by a continuous "spark" or power-conducting beam of particles or waves. This connection is the astral cord, and the tremendously high rate of the wave-form associated with the living entity maintains that connection. The projections cannot be prolonged, but sometimes I have returned to the physical body two or three times, as if to be "recharged."

90. "Life" is commonplace, we see it all around us; but every living thing is a combination of the physical and spiritual, and this is not common knowledge in the laboratory and elsewhere. The time spent in trying to find a physical reason for the flat-worm's memory will not solve the problem of the salmon's "memory" of its birthplace, nor physical reasoning that of homing or telepathy. The "sympathy" between identical twins when miles apart,

whose aches and pains or upsets are communicated, has often been reported, but the mystified relatives soon treat this as commonplace.

91. In recent years, research into the fundamental structure of matter has proved that "solid matter" is, in reality, no more "solid" than the spirit entities which are the subject of this treatise. The atoms have been found to consist of a bewildering number of "particles" which are nothing more than concentrations of energy. Matter and energy have proved to be interchangeable. The principles of wave-mechanics have revealed that the sub-atomic particles behave as though they were nothing more substantial than trains of electro-magnetic waves. The physical and the paraphysical sciences are rapidly approaching each other and the day cannot be far distant when they are recognized to be different aspects of the same system.

The Inspired Teachings of Zodiac
from The Greater World Association Trust

THE ZODIAC MESSAGES (Reference Edition) compiled and arranged by A. H. Hillyard

In this volume of 395 pages of actual text some 69 of Zodiac's most outstanding addresses on important subjects have been annotated and indexed for easy reading and study. They concern the great Scheme of Creation; the Evolution of the Soul; the Purpose of the Earthlife; Free-Will; Predestination, etc.; and are in simple language and terms easy to grasp. We commend this beautiful and inspiring book as your treasured companion.

THE ZODIAC MESSAGES (Non-Reference) Vol. 1 compiled by F. N. Tolkin

This book contains 30 Zodiac Addresses on important subjects: Auras; Animals; Suffering; Reincarnation; Christ the Judged; The Holy Spirit; Telepathy, etc.

THE ZODIAC MESSAGES (Non-Reference) Vol. 2 compiled by F. N. Tolkin

Companion to Vol. 1, contains 32 Zodiac Messages on, The Greater World of Spirit; The Friends of God; The Era of Revelation; The Uses of Adversity, etc. The above two books are beautiful and instructive.

THE PRAYERS OF ZODIAC compiled by A. H. Hillyard

In response to public demand a collection of Prayers of this wise Teacher have been produced in one volume. A blessing in one's private devotions, and to those who speak the word of God in public.

Christian Spiritualist Classics from:
The Greater World Association Trust

A BOOK OF SERVICES by A. H. Hillyard

Contains Orders of Services, with instructive notes, for use by ministers, pastors, and all who have charge of non-conformist churches.

THE GREEN LEAVES OF THE SPIRIT by A. H. Hillyard

The Green Leaves of the Spirit symbolise Life in its creative upward trend; for all life is of Spirit and stems from the one great source—God; by whom all things were made, and whose Spirit dwells within each and every one.

THE MINISTRY OF ANGELS by Joy Snell

A beautiful book dedicated to the Bereaved. Mrs. Snell was a hospital nurse and she describes her visions in the wards of Spirit helpers ministering to the sick.

THE LIFE BEYOND THE VEIL by the Rev. G. Vale Owen

Vol. 1 – The Lowlands of Heaven
Vol. 2 – The Highlands of Heaven
Vol. 3 – The Ministry of Heaven
Vol. 4 – The Battalions of Heaven
Vol. 5 – The Outlands of Heaven

Given by progressive Spirit communication through the hand of the Rev. G. Vale Owen in the vestry of his Church at Orford, Lancs. These books are classics of great spiritual beauty. They describe in these fascinating narratives life and progression in the Spheres Beyond.

PAUL AND ALBERT by the Rev. G. Vale Owen

What happens to those who have lived selfish, cruel and depraved lives on earth? Here, through the hand of the Rev. G. Vale Owen, is an authentic account of conditions that apply in these nether regions.

QUESTIONS YOU MAY BE ASKED by Winifred Moyes

The contents include such subjects as: Angels; Animals; Clairvoyance; Dreams, Fairies; etc.

SPIRITUAL REALMS by J. B. Wheatley

"The After Life Experience of a lawyer." This book adequately fills an hitherto unfortunate gap in our knowledge of the next world. It may well be that a communication on this subject has been delayed until sufficient people on earth could accept it.

BOOK LIST

A comprehensive Book List is available from the Greater World Association Book Room, 3 Lansdowne Road, Holland Park, London W11 3AL, England.

PUBLICATIONS

The Greater World: A weekly Spiritualist journal based on the Christ Teachings.

The Childrens Greater World: A Monthly magazine for children of all ages, useful for the home and Sunday School.

Specimen copies sent on request.

The Greater World Association Trust,
3 Lansdowne Road, Holland Park, London W11 3AL, England.